Sunset
SWIMMING
POOLS

By the Editors of Sunset Books and Sunset Magazine

Lane Books · Menlo Park, California

Edited by Phyllis Elving

Special Consultant: Betty Clinton

ACKNOWLEDGMENTS

Our thanks to all the members of the National Swimming Pool Institute; to special consultants J. Henry Mohr and Donald W. Smiley of Nor-Cal Engineering Co., Inc.; to the Swimming Pool Industry Council of California; and to all of the swimming pool companies and contractors for their cooperation and guidance.

PHOTOGRAPHERS

WILLIAM APLIN: 32, 35, 44 top. APLIN-DUDLEY STUDIOS: 18 top, 39 bottom, 47 bottom. MORLEY BAER: 65 top. ERNEST BRAUN: 13 top, 17 bottom left and right, 19, 31 bottom, 47 top left and right, 49, 57 bottom right. WILLIAM CARTER: 25, 84-85, 87, 88, 99 top and bottom, 100 all photos, 101. ROBERT C. CLEVELAND: 30 bottom. ROBERT COX: 18 bottom. GLENN CHRISTIANSEN: 15 top, 22-23, 24, 36-37, 38 bottom, 43 bottom, 45 bottom, 51 top, 52 bottom, 59 bottom right. RICHARD DAWSON: 5 bottom, 61 top. MAX ECKERT: 8 bottom, 20 top, 33 top. PHYLLIS ELVING: 70. RICHARD FISH: 4 top, 13 bottom, 17 top, 21 bottom, 29 bottom, 30 top right, 41 all photos, 43 top, 46 bottom, 59 top, 106. FRANK L. GAYNOR: 76 top. GENERAL ELECTRIC COMPANY: 56. HALLMARK POOL CORPORATION: 96 left. HOFFMAN PUBLICATIONS: 21 top. BOB IACOPI: 12 left and right, 34 bottom, 91 top. ROY KRELL: 38 top. MAJOR POOL EQUIPMENT CORPORATION: 53 bottom, 83, 93 left and right, 94 all photos. ORVILLE MARSH: 91 bottom. ELLS MARUGG: 11 bottom. MASTER POOLS BY FIESTA POOLS: 20 bottom. JACK McDOWELL: 66-67, 68, 75, 78, 79, 80, 102-103, 104, 105 top. DON NORMARK: 4 bottom, 10 top, 31 top. KENT OPPENHEIMER: 26 top left, 26 bottom. PADDOCK POOL CONSTRUCTION COMPANY: 26 top right. POOLS BY RAPP: 6-7. PETE REDPATH: 57 bottom left, 62-63, 65 bottom. KARL H. RIEK: 28. JOHN ROBINSON: 34 top. ROTHSCHILD PHOTO: 60. SAN JUAN POOLS: 97. JULIUS SHULMAN: 39 top. DOUGLAS SIMMONDS: 54-55. SHAN STEWART: 29 top. SUN/FUN POOL ENCLOSURES: 50. DARROW WATT: 14, 30 top left, 40, 42, 48 top, 53 top left and right, 58, 59 bottom left, 76 bottom left and right. WEATHER KING PRODUCTS, INC.: 15 bottom. ELTON WELKE: 96 right. R. WENKAM: 8 top, 11 top, 57 top, 44 bottom. MASON WEYMOUTH: 10 bottom. GEORGE WOO: 61 bottom.

FRONT COVER: Black plaster was used to finish walls and bottom of freeform pool to heighten water's reflective quality. Decking has seeded pebble finish. Landscape designer: Philip S. Grimes. Photograph by William Carter.

Fourth Printing December 1971

CONTENTS

SPECIAL FEATURES

PAVING directs you naturally from house to pool and garden beyond; patio has built-in seating. Landscape architect: Kenneth K. Hayashi.

MIRRORLIKE quality of desert pool results from black pigment in surfacing of sides and bottom. Any water that splashes out flows over concrete apron, sinks into desert sand. Landscape architect: Guy Greene.

OCTAGONAL pavilion ove circular pool. Cedar board leads to pool deck of same ma Landscape architect: Roy F

A PRIVATE SWIMMING POOL

Pools specifically built for bathing are known to have existed as long ago as 3000 B.C. But not until the creation of the grand and complex pools of Rome did swimming become a recreational activity.

Swimming pools in the form of public plunges and health spas enjoyed a surge of popularity during the mid-nineteenth century. In the early 1900's, only a privileged few could afford to build or even own private pools. Today, however, a private swimming pool is not an uncommon luxury.

Sunset's first edition of *Swimming Pools* was published in 1959. At that time, new construction methods had helped to lower installation costs considerably so that owning a private swimming pool was no longer restricted to the wealthy. Since then a rise in population and income, combined with changing attitudes and increased suburban living, has accelerated the desire for swimming pools so greatly that by 1969 nearly a million in-ground pools had been installed in the United States.

The swimming pool industry has undergone considerable changes. New techniques of construction have been developed, standards have been formed, and extensive chemical research has been conducted. The potential pool owner can choose from a wide selection of pool styles and types. Reliable contractors, because of strong competition, have learned to work closely with the customer to achieve complete satisfaction.

Despite the increasing demand for and availability of pools, many people discover that acquiring and owning one involves a great deal more than they had expected. The intent of this book is to provide the information a pool owner needs. The book goes into the various aspects of owning a swimming pool, from planning it to maintaining and enjoying it.

FREEFORM pool with miniature waterfall and rock coping, backed by garden, presents a serene view from inside the house. Decking extends up to the pool on the house side, integrating house and pool.

BASICS OF PLANNING

A body of water as large as a swimming pool will dominate most garden and patio areas. Activities will revolve around the pool and change the traffic pattern of the entire home. Even in the off-season for swimming, the pool is an important visual part of a garden. Therefore the importance of thorough planning cannot be overstressed.

Because of the great variety in pool shapes and sizes, perhaps the greatest challenge in planning for a pool is in choosing the best design to fit your budget and your property. Proper design must meet demands that will arise during the entire lifetime of your pool. Will the size and shape of the pool be adequate for your family both now and in ten years? Will its size, shape, and location help or hinder resale of the house? Is the equipment long-lasting, or will it require considerable maintenance or replacement within a few years? Is the pool given the prominence it deserves, yet located so it will not over-run all other phases of outdoor living?

Use the check list on page 110 as a guide to help you evaluate what type of pool, accessories, and poolside features best fit your requirements.

SELECTING A SITE

To select the proper site for your pool, first be sure your property is suitable for a below-grade structure; then locate the pool where it will be most enjoyable and practical. For advice, consult a landscape architect or a competent swimming pool representative.

Can you dig?

In-ground swimming pools range from 3 feet to as deep as 12 feet (plus an allowance around the shell for backfill). A pool must be fitted into an area clear of underground utility obstructions such as drainage, gas, and water lines and telephone and power conduits. Existing or abandoned septic tanks, walls, or other structures that might impede excavation can

also limit the space available for a pool. Rerouting utility lines, relocating necessary structures, or removing obstructions may be impossible or extremely expensive.

As most cities and counties consider a pool to be an auxiliary structure, a building permit is required. Your local building and health departments can advise you on set-back and fencing laws, health standards, and the number of inspections required during construction. Check the deed to your house, as it may contain restrictions on building and define easements for power and telephone installations.

Investigating for these construction limitations and taking any necessary remedial action is up to the pool owner, not the city or pool contractor. When you contract a pool builder, he will assume that your property has been cleared for excavation and construction of a below-grade pool.

If your property cannot be excavated for a full in-ground pool, inquire about an above-ground installa-tion (see page 14). Some of these pools are designed with a deep-end that requires only minor exca-vation. Some require no excavation at all.

Water around the pool

Good drainage is crucial around a swimming pool. A pool can be weakened, cracked, or even pushed out of the ground if water collects under it and builds up pressure. If your garden is not in a natural drain-age area, a drainage system must be provided at the base of the pool. Consult the contractor who builds the pool or the engineer who draws up the plans; he can recommend a drainage system which can be installed at the time of excavation.

In all cases, deck areas must be designed to carry water away from the pool. Decking should be sloped ¼ inch to the foot, downgrade from the pool. At a natural breaking point, a drain line may be installed to move the water into a natural drainage channel.

SMALL POOL is set close to house on narrow lot between road and beach. House wall was converted to sliding screens and panels to form lanai-pavilion. Architects: Lemmon, Freeth, Haines & Jones.

TO SEPARATE pool and patio areas, pool was placed above terrace level. Designers: Armstrong & Sharfman.

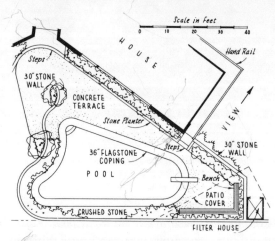

FREEFORM pool fits into triangle below level of hillside house. Patio roof shelters a corner.

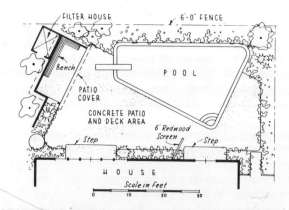

SHAPE OF POOL set in small lot permits large deck. Bench and barbecue area are covered by patio roof.

Allowance for access

Before excavation can begin, there must be adequate access for heavy equipment. The minimum amount of access width to the pool site is 6 to 8 feet, though 10 feet is preferable. Small equipment can be brought in through a space 5 to 5½ feet wide, at additional cost to the home owner, but anything less than 5 feet means the pool must be hand-dug, at prohibitive costs.

Fences and plantings may have to be removed. And if a portion of a patio, driveway, or lawn must be crossed by heavy equipment, some damage is likely to occur.

The location of the pool

Back yards usually are the largest and most private areas available, but other possible pool locations should not be ignored. A space between a front gate and house wing, a side yard, or an awkward corner that sometimes shows up in a subdivision lot may be more suitable to give your family maximum enjoyment with minimum upkeep.

In some communities you may have a pool in the front, between house and street, providing it is properly fenced. In other areas you may apply through the offices of the building inspector or planning commissioner for a variance allowing you to install a pool in front.

Whatever the location, for the most ideal arrangement you should consider the amount of sun the pool will receive, the exposure to wind, the view presented by the pool from within your house, and the space needed around the pool for activity and storage areas.

Sunshine and shade. The pool should receive maximum sun during the swimming season and be free of shade during the hours of greatest use. If a diving board is to be installed, the deep end of the pool should be oriented so divers leave the board with their backs to the sun, rather than facing direct glare.

Some shade around the pool is welcome for entertaining, barbecuing, and lounging. If naturally shaded areas are not available where you want them, a cabana or patio roof can be added later (see section on Poolside Structures and Fences, page 36).

Protection from wind. Summer breezes can become chilly around a swimming pool. Wind will also steal heat from the water's surface, and unless its main force is controlled it will cause your pool heater to work overtime to make up for the loss.

Fences and the house itself may control the wind sufficiently, but if they do not, try to incorporate a permanent or portable windbreak in your plans. A decorative wind screen often can serve as a safety fence.

Wind propels leaves and other debris over the surface of the water, so the pool will be easier to clean if the skimmer outlet is located on the downwind side of the pool.

The view from inside. Many people use a pool as a centerpiece for their entire landscaping plan, preferring to have it as visible as possible from inside the house. Others would rather the pool be out of sight. If children are around, full view of the water is a distinct advantage; mothers can then look outside and see in an instant where the youngsters are playing.

Try to locate the pool so that reflections from the rising or setting sun will not shine directly into the house. When this cannot be avoided, screens can help reduce the glare.

If your property has a natural view, you may be able to use natural backdrops as a frame for the pool area. Distant mountains, forested areas, or even city landscapes can extend the visual impact of the pool beyond your property lines.

Space around the pool. When you build a pool, it becomes a focus for outdoor activities. Most outdoor entertaining will revolve around it. But space design should allow for traffic patterns in other areas of a patio or garden as well and should provide areas for non-swimmers to relax without getting splashed.

For ease of cleaning, locate the pool as far away from trees and large shrubs as the area permits. No matter how well you plan, debris will enter your pool, but overhanging trees especially create a maintenance problem. Leaves and, worse, fruit from a crop-bearing tree can stain the pool wall surfaces and color the water.

Children's sandboxes, gravel areas, and similar sources of debris should be some distance from the pool; wet feet tend to track substantial amounts of dirt into the water.

Provision for pool equipment. A basic part of the swimming pool is the filter and pump; a heater will add another piece of equipment. Efficiency of operation is the primary concern when determining the site of pool equipment. If possible, it should be located near the deep end of the pool to assure short pipe runs for the recirculating system.

The equipment must be installed on a concrete slab, preferably not underground and not more than 2 feet above grade level. Filters will stand 3 to 4 feet high, heaters even higher, depending upon the type you purchase. Proper drainage must be available for backwashing the filter system (see section on filtering system, page 102).

If it is impractical to locate the equipment behind a fence, garage corner, or similar structure, you can hide it with an attractive shelter or plant screen.

HUGE BOULDERS shelter desert pool; flagstone coping and paving with texture and color similar to native rock enhance the way the pool fits naturally into its site.

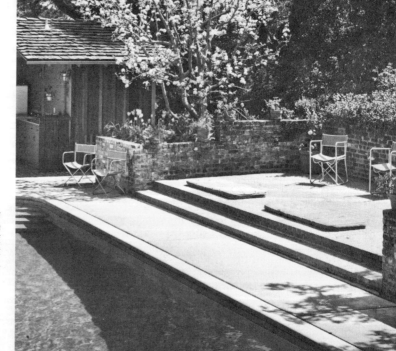

SUN POCKET was created by raised brick plant beds cut into the hillside near the shallow end of this pool. Roofed shelter at left has fireplace, sink, dressing rooms.

GRACEFUL POOL and ocean beyond make water the most important element of the view from within this house. Fence screens pool and garden from drive without blocking view of ocean.

REDWOOD-FRAMED glass screen stops the wind, lets in the view, and keeps young children from pool area when they can't be supervised. Two large sections of the screen slide open; simple lock is out of children's reach.

CONSTRUCTING A HILLSIDE POOL

Many attractive pools are situated on hillsides, but these can be the most troublesome and expensive sites of all. Engineering costs will exceed those for a flat lot, and you will be limited in selection of size, shape, and type of construction. Nevertheless, competent builders have developed new construction techniques for seemingly impossible sites.

A hillside pool must withstand earth pressure on one side and have well-engineered support on the other. Down-slope supports for the pool should be built on a solid foundation, preferably rock. Retaining walls on the up-slope side, sometimes incorporating the pool structure itself, must be sufficient to contain a possible earth or loose-rock slide.

Surface water must be routed from the hill around the pool to a lower slope, and decks must be designed to prevent water from seeping into the ground near the pool.

There are no standard rules for hillside pool construction. Take the time to seek out companies and contractors with a reputation for tackling tough problems. A soil report and possibly a geologist's report may be needed before construction can begin.

Pool access and adequate decking can be a real challenge. It is a good idea to start by planning the area completely on paper, including all steps, decking, and structures. If the area is too confined or construction too expensive, a pool may be altogether impractical.

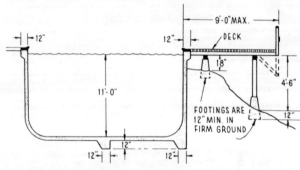

POOL AND DECK of redwood project out over steep bank. Pool is gunite, 11 feet deep to insure firm footing in solid ground; exposed wall is extra thick. Deck is separate to minimize strain. Designer: Harry Dyke.

DECK EXTENDS level area of pool terrace out over steep hillside. Posts standing on cylindrical concrete piers support the deck, and natural vegetation conceals understructure from down-slope neighbors. Landscape architect: Anthony Guzzardo.

ONE CORNER of freeform pool is partly free standing, and the deck is built out over the steep bank. Pump, filter, and heater are beneath deck. High wall at left serves as one side of pool. Landscape architect: Joseph Copp, Jr.

ABOVE-GROUND SWIMMING POOLS

Prefabricated above-ground swimming pools have recently become a popular alternative to in-ground installations. Over 3,000,000 above-ground pools are in use today in the United States. Their popularity has increased steadily as manufacturers have extended the variety of sizes and designs available.

These pools range from the basic "tank" type with equal depth throughout (usually 4 feet) to models that include perimeter decking and either a sloping bottom or deep-end hopper requiring a partial excavation. Sizes vary from 12-foot-diameter circular pools to 20 by 40-foot rectangles. Shapes are limited to circles, ovals, and rectangles.

Construction material usually consists of durable galvanized steel or aluminum walls with interior vinyl liners. The outer panels may feature attractive color designs. Decking ranges from a side-top rim for seating to a fully fenced-in area around the pool, wide enough to include patio furniture.

Prices for above-ground pools vary from less than $500 for the minimum-sized, equal-depth pools, to a cost approximately the same as a small in-ground pool for the large, fully-decked models.

Filter units, either sand or diatomaceous earth, are specially designed for this type of pool. Skimmers are floating lily-pad units or in some cases are recessed into the wall structure. Maintenance chores are simple, and the pools can be easily winterized.

The height of the pool from the ground is a built-in safety feature. Removable ladders or access steps that swing out of reach effectively keep children from the area when the pool is not in use.

Installing an above-ground pool from a pool kit can be an enjoyable family project. The pool can be disassembled and removed to a new location, an added attraction for mobile families. Since these structures are considered portable, many communities do not require that they be included in the owner's property tax assessment.

FROM ABOVE you wouldn't know this pool is a prefabricated, above-ground model. Bottom of vinyl-lined pool rests on cushion of sandy loam. Poolhouse at back is partly below deck.

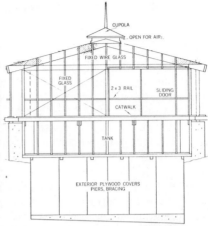

UP-IN-THE-TREETOPS pool is a vinyl-lined 21-foot-diameter redwood water tank on base of piers and bracing. Glass enclosure and deck are independent of tank structure; heater, filter are under decking.
Architect: Jack Hermann.

RECTANGULAR above-ground pool is vinyl-lined aluminum, has narrow decking with one wide end to accommodate patio furniture. Safety fence comes with the pool kit.

DETERMINING THE POOL'S SIZE AND SHAPE

Cost and available space will help you determine the size and shape of your pool. But personal preferences and the ways in which you will use your pool are the most important considerations.

Cost

The cost of a swimming pool is determined by the area in which you live, the type of construction and condition of the site, and the size and shape of the pool. (See guide to Pool Construction, page 84.) In general, irregular shapes require more wall surface than do straight lines. However, a simple kidney or teardrop design can cost less, since the rounded corners and inside curves result in less actual perimeter feet. All price estimates you obtain should specify the actual perimeter of the pool, in addition to its maximum dimensions and square footage.

Many pool builders have established a variety of basic shapes as "standards" in their array of models. It is possible to modify a standard shape slightly without too much additional cost, but a complete departure into a freeform "lake" design will raise the price considerably.

Available space

The most reliable way to find out what size pool will fit on your property is to measure the available space yourself with a tape measure. Here are a few tips to remember:

• Unless you are building a pool with abnormal proportions, figure the width as just less than half the length.

• Surface dimensions are deceiving. A 20 by 40-foot rectangle is just that. But for a kidney shape, for example, a "20-foot" width will be 20 feet at its widest point and 16 or 17 feet at the neck.

• Allow for coping and decking. A minimum of 3 feet of walkway (including coping) is usually recommended around the edge of the pool. A 16 by 32-foot kidney shape without diving board needs 38 feet of length and 22 feet of width at its widest point. If a diving board is to be installed, extra decking will be required. A 20 by 40-foot rectangular pool with a diving board needs a minimum area of 26 by 54 feet.

• Allowance should be planned for patios and activity areas near the pool.

Personal requirements

Your pool should be planned as an integrated part of your landscaping, patio, house, and land contours. You may wish to call in a landscape architect for advice on the best shape of pool for your property. A formal garden might be matched with a formal pool, a natural setting with a free-flowing design. The home owner who decides to select his own size and shape will do best to stick to the conventional forms unless lot obstructions dictate otherwise.

Before you can decide on a shape and position for your pool, you must decide what uses your pool is likely to have, now and in the future. It may be a recreation spot for casual relaxation of adults, a playground for children, or perhaps a training ground for competitive swimmers and divers. If the pool will be used mostly by small children and non-swimming adults, the shallow end should be the broadest. With children, however, future needs must be considered. As children learn to swim, they will quickly outgrow a pool designed primarily for shallow-end activity or one with a special wading area.

Of all dimensions, the depth of your pool deserves the most attention. Three feet is recommended as the minimum depth, but even non-swimmers prefer 3½ to 5 feet. Racing and turning requires a 3½-foot depth; divers must have at least 8½ but preferably 9 feet of unobstructed depth. If a diving board is installed, the width of the pool should be at least 15 feet, and the distance from the deep-end wall to the 5-foot "breaking point" should be at least 22 feet.

If you plan your swimming pool as a training ground for competitive swimming, it helps if the length is an even divisor of 75 feet — usually 25 or 37½ feet. Swimmers in training can then establish a style that will be usable for competitive meets in a 75-foot A.A.U. pool. Competitive diving requires a minimum depth of 9 feet for a board 1 meter above the surface of the water (12 feet for a 3-meter board) and a minimum of 15 feet of head room.

Resale value

The possibility that you may sell your property after a pool has been installed may affect pool design. An odd-shaped pool may not attract potential buyers.

The standard rectangles, kidneys, teardrops, wedges, and L-shapes are the most popular pool designs. If you do decide on a freeform, be sure it fits the house and landscaping as well as being suitable for your family. Good landscaping designs are good selling points, but peculiarities are not. A pool smaller than 450 square feet or larger than 800 may hamper resale. Too small a pool is not adequate for a growing family, and the maintenance costs of a large pool may discourage other buyers.

It is a good idea to have the pool designed for diving, whether you will use a diving board or not. Anchors for the diving board can be installed in the deck when the pool is constructed and then covered with a thin layer of cement. If new owners decide to install a board, the cement is easily chipped away.

Gleaming chrome accessories, an underwater light, or a ladder can be good selling points.

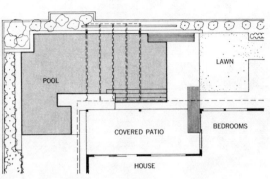

POOL WRAPS around corner of roofed patio in 20-foot-deep rear yard, its 34-foot length occupying about half of former lawn area. Jet massage section, left foreground, is set apart by diving peninsula. Landscape architects: Jones and Peterson.

DIVING AND SHALLOW areas are separated by deep-end offset of pool at left and peninsula in pool at right. Landscape architects: Eckbo, Royston & Williams (left), Thomas Church (right).

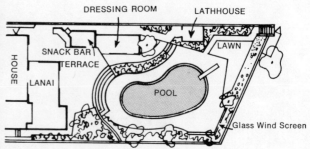

POOL, LATHHOUSE, snack bar, dressing room, and lanai all fit on 50-foot lot. Curves of pool and landscaping create sense of space. Glass wall stops wind without hiding view. Landscape architect: Ruth Shellhorn.

CUT STONE coping and freeform shape of this pool create a pondlike appearance against the background of a wooded hill. Designer: Kathryn Stedman.

MODIFIED rectangle shape has wide brick steps leading into water at shallow end. Precast coping stones were used around rest of pool. Landscape architect: Thomas Church.

POPULAR POOL SHAPES

Among the most popular swimming pool shapes are circles, rectangles, teardrops, kidneys, L-shapes, and freeforms. Each has its advantages, and your personal preferences and space limitations will determine what shape is best for you.

• The circle is easily adapted to small yards. Often this shape is used for shallow wading pools, but circle pools can be deep enough for diving.

• The rectangle is best for competitive swimming and is available in several construction materials.

• The teardrop fits into most gardens. A similar shape is the oval, with each end the same size.

• The kidney is perhaps the most popular shape. Its curves can be modified to fit the particular site, and it works with most landscaping.

• The L-shape fits easily into a corner or around a house projection. Diving and swimming areas are defined by the pool shape.

• Freeform pools are best for crowded yards or irregular areas, since the shape can be designed to fit the available space.

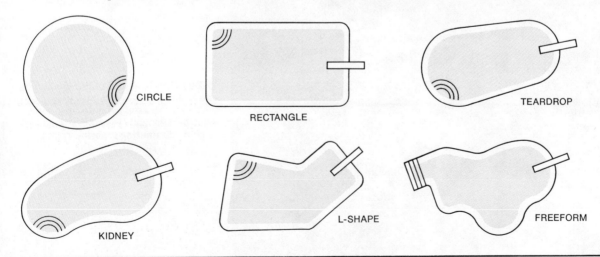

CIRCLE   RECTANGLE   TEARDROP

KIDNEY   L-SHAPE   FREEFORM

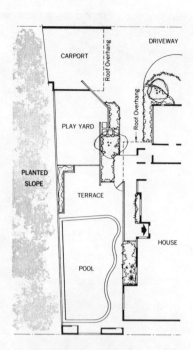

CURVED LINES soften look of pool in narrow area between house and rear slope. Terrace for sunbathing and entertaining is separated by a wall from a children's play yard. Designers: Armstrong & Sharfman.

WIDE STEPS lead into shallow end of 20 by 50-foot freeform pool which curves around landscaped area. Wide deck extends to water around rest of pool, eliminating separate coping.

SYMMETRY of curved and straight lines gives this pool a classical look. Basic shape is rectangular, with semicircles at each end. Wall around patio repeats curves of pool.

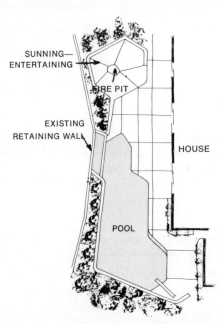

POOL FITS seemingly impossible site between house and retaining wall at base of rear slope. An exposed aggregate wall now forms limits of two sides of pool, has hand-toe slots. Landscape architects: Donald Brinkerhoff and Associates.

SUNNING—
ENTERTAINING

FIRE PIT

EXISTING
RETAINING WALL

HOUSE

POOL

BRICK COPING blends well with clay containers used in the landscaping of this pool. Raised wooden deck areas on either side are joined visually by overhead beams. Sitting area in center foreground opens from glass-walled living room.

POOL TRIMMING AND LANDSCAPING

Opportunities for individual expression in the design of your pool usually are greatest in the selection of trim, accessories, decking, and plants. Trim and accessories make up the "face" of the pool, while paving and decks contribute texture and color and form a transition zone between the water and other parts of the garden. Strategic planting unites the entire pool and patio area visually.

TRIM AND ACCESSORIES

A pool, like a house, can suffer either from lack of design and color or from a hodge-podge of conflicting colors and gleaming chrome. Don't be afraid to try new ideas, but use some restraint in combining decorative elements.

The list of accessories given here is by no means exhaustive; new specialty items are constantly being developed. Your pool company, contractor, or an equipment company can provide you with the latest information on accessories, including their prices and their adaptability to your pool.

Interior finish

The interior finish of your pool — paint, plaster, vinyl, or fiberglass — determines what you see when you look into the pool. Correctly maintained water is clear, and the color of the surface behind it will control the apparent color of the water.

White is the customary color for a pool finish. Against white, clear pool water reflects the blue of the sky and takes on a sparkle. Light blue or green finishes tend to make the water look tinted. Black or dark gray is used occasionally, both to create dramatic reflections and to help raise water temperature by retaining natural heat from the sun.

Plaster can be colored before being applied to the

pool surface. Aqua and light blue are most often used in vinyl and fiberglass pools, though white and other colors are obtainable.

A variety of paint colors is available, and some imaginative designers have used them to create multi-colored patterns on pool interiors.

Tile

Tile is often used as trim around the water line. It conceals daily fluctuations in the water level, and the scum line that invariably forms is easily cleaned from its surface. Tile is also usable in other areas of the pool — on the risers of the steps, in patterns in the walls or floor, and around an underwater light niche.

A popular form of tile is mosaic — tiny pieces of ceramic in square, rectangular, or irregular shapes, separated by grout and installed in a band around the water line. This type of tile allows an almost infinite variety of color and design.

Tile can also be set in single or double rows of 6-inch squares, either in one color or with decorative tiles set in a color design. Some designers recommend that 3 by 6-inch "soldier" tile be used to add an extra element of texture to the trim.

Light blue is the color usually recommended for tile, since it adds blue tints to the water. Contrasting colors or bright hues can give the pool a custom touch and match colors used in decking, fences, or auxiliary buildings.

Coping

Coping is the lip of the pool, the edging that provides a non-skid walking surface and hand-hold around the edge of the water. It also can form a visual transition between pool and landscaping. Coping stones are used on all pools except those of steel and aluminum (where the edging is fabricated of the same material), most poured pools (where the coping is poured as a contiguous part of the bond beam), and some above-ground pools. Coping is fabricated as part of the structure in fiberglass one-piece shell pools, although other types of edging can be installed right on top of the fiberglass if you wish.

Coping is usually thought of as the precast stones that are set on most pools; they are practical and present no rough edges above the water. Coping materials do vary, however. Concrete, brick, or flagstone are common alternatives. And if standard coping doesn't blend with the paving around the pool, many pool owners prefer to expand the paving to include the coping.

The precast stones are available in a wide range of colors, in custom combinations of pastel backgrounds and bright exposed color chips which form a terrazzo-like finish, or in simulated natural rock forms. One precast coping forms a pebbled surface which remains cool on hot days.

Diving board

Of all accessories, a diving board is probably the most popular. A board can be installed on all pools 30 feet or more in length that have a depth of at least 8 ½ feet.

There are three main types of diving boards that can be used with residential pools: laminated Douglas fir encased in fiberglass-reinforced plastic; high tensile, laminated fiberglass cloth with rigid wood stringers; and extruded aluminum. The laminated fiberglass boards are extremely durable and very strong, and they have a built-in finish. Aluminum

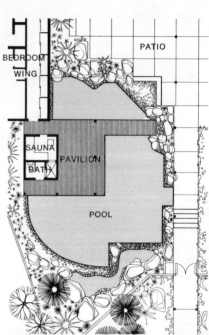

SMOOTH ROCK coping gives natural effect; pool interior is painted black for reflecting quality. Pond at bottom in drawing is separate from main pool. Pavilion contains sauna, rests above water on piers, is connected by bridge to main patio. Pavilion architect: Frank Robert. Landscape architect: Richard Tongg.

boards are the most permanent and require the least upkeep.

Prices vary considerably. For a 12-foot board, fiberglass-laminated fir is $115 to $130, high tensile fiberglass approximately $130, and aluminum $225 to $300. Boards are available in 8, 10, 12, 14, and 16-foot lengths; boards of 10 or 12 feet are the most practical for residential pools.

Special apparatus is available for pools deep enough for diving but too limited in deck space for a diving board. Jump boards are built of the same materials as regular diving boards but are only 4 to 8 feet long and rest on a heavy-duty spring bolted to the deck. Portable diving trampolines are very small, square trampolines mounted on metal legs.

Ladder and grab rails

Ladders are useful in vinyl liner pools, where no steps are constructed, and in large pools where deep-end access is desired. Ladders are set in the deck with anchors and must be planned when the pool is constructed. Stainless steel and chrome-plated brass are the only materials now commonly used for ladders in residential pools. Chrome-plated brass is attractive and easily polished, but it will not withstand heavy use as well as stainless steel. A ladder of stainless steel will have a longer life than chrome-plated brass and still take a good polish after many years.

Costs are about $70 to $115 for a three-tread and $80 to $140 for a four-tread ladder. Anchors for ladders are an additional $6 to $20 apiece; two are required for each ladder.

Grab rails are an increasingly popular alternative to the pool ladder. Two rails, shaped somewhat like the top of a pool ladder, are anchored into the deck to give the swimmer a hand-hold as he climbs out of the water on glazed ceramic treads imbedded in the pool wall. Rails are made of aluminum, stainless steel, or chrome-plated brass and are less costly than ladders. Prices range from $40 to $90 for the rails with anchors and $6 to $15 for a set of three inset steps.

Grab rails are not as susceptible to corrosion as ladders, since no metal extends into the water. Treads do require extra thick pool wall and special steel reinforcement at the place where they are imbedded.

GRAB RAILS and a slide are among accessories installed for this pool. Foot treads are imbedded in pool wall. Mosaic tile trim forms a band around the top of the pool.

PALOS VERDES stone forms wall along two sides of pool. Accessories include pedestal diving board, ladder.

'GREEK' pool has 10-foot diving board, grab rails, tile trim, coping stones, textured deck area.

THERAPEUTIC pool at one end of main pool has auxiliary pump, special jets on direct lines from heater. Water bubbles into pool at 90-95°, splashes over dividing wall into main pool before it reaches returns.

Underwater lighting

An underwater light gives attractive colors to a pool at night and provides an added safety feature — most underwater lights yield sufficient illumination to clearly show the pool's outline at night. Some pool ladders come with built-in lights, eliminating the need for a separate pool light.

Check with local building codes before selecting an underwater light. The National Electric Code specifies several acceptable systems, any one of which might be adopted in your area. A popular system recommended by the NEC uses 110-volt lighting fixtures with built-in ground detection devices that sense any leakage and break the connection. You are thereby automatically protected should the system malfunction.

Another method is a low-voltage (12-volt) system that uses specially designed 300 to 500-watt bulbs. This is the most expensive, since it requires the use of a transformer mounted away from the pool.

The NEC specifies that the inside bottom of the junction boxes for 110-volt systems be mounted 8 inches above pool deck, grade, or water level, and at least 4 feet away from the pool. Metallic niches for the lights often are mandatory, to be installed at least 18 inches below the normal water line.

Wet-niche lights are almost universally used; dry-niche lights can be a hazard if the lens is broken.

One safety device available for pools with high-voltage lighting has an isolating transformer (110 volts) connected to a circuit breaker. The circuit breaker instantly cuts off the electricity whenever a short or ground occurs.

Pool markers

A rope lifeline is useful to mark the shallow end reserved for children, indicate the beginning of the diving area, or mark off swimming lanes. The rope is hooked onto wall mountings installed when the pool is constructed or attached to deck anchors.

Polyethylene or nylon rope (40 to 95 cents a foot) is best, since it is little affected by constant immersion in water. Hooks ($2 to $5 apiece) are needed on each end of the rope for attaching it to the anchors ($2 to $9 depending on type of mounting). For added safety and to mark line location, plastic floats ($1 to $3 apiece) usually are attached to the rope at 3 or 4-foot intervals.

Pool covers

Covers for swimming pools keep winter debris out of the water, cut down on chemical requirements, reduce algae growth, eliminate long hours with the leaf skimmer, and (if strong enough) serve as safety devices.

Pool covers need not be elaborate. Even a large sheet of inexpensive black polyethylene (good for one or two seasons), floating on the water's surface and anchored at the edges by 2 by 4's or rocks, affords some protection.

A fitted vinyl or nylon cover will hold up more satisfactorily and look much better. Some covers of this type are held down with deck anchor plates; others are tied to anchors set in the soil, or even to low-profile plates cemented to the deck with epoxy cement. Still another type is anchored with water-filled tubes.

The material used in the cover should be resistant to water, weather, and pool chemicals. If the material is porous, rain water will pass through, leaving no stagnant, dirty lake on top of the cover. Solid covers can be equipped with grommet drains.

On larger pools, plastic covers sometimes sag in the middle. They can be supported either by poles laid across the water or by inner tubes floated under the cover at strategic points.

The most expensive covers — but also the safest, most attractive, and easiest to use — are the rigid models mounted on tracks, bars, or metal supports. Motor-driven units are available, at $1000 or more.

The safety feature afforded by the better plastic covers is not foolproof. A youngster can loosen most of them. Covers also can be punctured by sharp edges or by the toenails of an inquisitive dog.

Therapeutic pools

One of the most popular additions to the private swimming pool is the built-in therapeutic spa. You first relax in the higher temperatures of the spa, then plunge in the cooler water of the pool for a stimulating swim. The water therapy units should be installed at the time of pool construction.

The most basic arrangement consists of an underwater step or bench for sitting, with hydro-air jets located below water level in the side wall of the pool (see photo, page 17). High-velocity aerated water flows from the jets, imparting massage-like water actions.

The fully implemented units are separated from the swimming pool by a dam, low enough to allow water from the therapeutic unit to spill over into the main pool, and have their own main drain. Underwater decks provide seating space for several people at a time; hydro-air jets encircle the area, and the water can be heated to whatever temperature is desired, usually from 90° to 108°. Some of these pools are operated directly from the swimming pool filter and heater system by special control valves, but most have an auxiliary pump and heater plus an inlet line from the main filter system.

PAVING AND DECKS

The deck area around a swimming pool serves a dual purpose. Functionally, it provides a safe walkway for swimmers and a necessary drainage surface. Aesthetically, it creates a frame for the pool. Be generous with decking; poolside furniture and lounging swimmers take up a surprising amount of space.

Traditionally, a pool has been surrounded by a rim of coping stone, then a 3 or 4-foot-wide strip of concrete, and then plants of some kind. The most common digression from the old-fashioned pattern is to eliminate the coping stone and extend the decking right to the water's edge. This technique helps eliminate the "bathtub" look; the smooth, uninterrupted poolside surface draws the eye to the water, integrating pool and garden.

Another variation is to arrange the concrete unevenly around the pool, as shown on the cover of this book. The larger areas lend themselves well to use as activity centers, and the pool area appears larger and more natural than if the paving were distributed in an even ribbon on all sides.

Plain concrete has gone by the wayside in this era of imaginative landscaping. Brushed or textured concrete and pebbled surfaces are very common. Though the costs are higher, colors are used in concrete to complement the water, tile, and coping; warm earth colors enhance the blue tint of the water and seem natural in a garden. Colors also help take glare off concrete. But keep in mind that dark colors absorb heat and can become very hot on sunny days.

Where summers are particularly hot, investigate "cool deck" products, designed to keep surfaces cool.

Wood decking can be used as raised sunning decks or as architectural extensions of concrete areas. Wood is often the only usable material in hillside situations (see pages 12 and 13). Bricks have a pleasing form and texture, used either in large quantities or just to soften large areas of concrete. Crushed rock is hard on bare feet, but it is very good for keeping the dust down and forming a drainage barrier between pool water and plants.

If you have existing patio or walkway areas that become slippery when wet, they can be treated with a solution of aluminum oxide mixed with waterproof paint or a clear compound. This will sufficiently roughen the texture of the surface to eliminate any slipping. The solution is sold at hardware stores and chemical companies under several brand names.

CANTILEVERED DECK extends over steep hill, is connected by bridge to house side. Architect: John Hans Ostwald.

FLAGSTONE flanks pool on hillside lot, and wood decking continues level space over slope. Irregularly-shaped stones relieve rigid geometric lines. Designer: Zareh Kiragh.

DECK EXTENDS house floor level to pool. Stained resawn Douglas fir 2 by 3's with chamfered (beveled) edges were used. Architect: Alfred T. Wilkes.

PEBBLES pressed in concrete deck at left were exposed by brushing, washing; those at right were set deep for smooth surface. Landscape architects: Robert Babcock (left), Joseph Copp, Jr. (right).

BRICKS can be used to create handsome decks, either just as walkway around pool or continued as patio floor. For this pool, concrete pads were used for patio. Designers: Eckbo, Royston & Williams.

ANGULAR shadow patterns of the surrounding desert were repeated in the shape of the paving around this pool. Pebbled deck leads to raised sitting area. For another view of pool, see page 4.

NATURAL FLAGSTONE was used to cover the entire deck area around this pool. Flagstone, waterfall at far left, and freeform shape of pool create a mountain lake atmosphere.

PLANTING AROUND THE POOL

If you've ever had to clean leaves, twigs, pine needles, or flower petals from a pool, you will understand why most pool owners don't want to plant anything next to the pool. Careful selection of plants and location of planting beds can keep maintenance chores to a minimum, and you can still create an attractive garden.

Plants near the pool

Too much chlorine will damage plants quickly, but a small amount won't be detrimental unless chlorinated water remains on the leaves of plants. Most landscape architects design wide deck areas or raised beds to protect plants, although limited plantings of hardy materials such as small palms, yucca, and horsetail sometimes can be located next to the pool. Plants in containers also can be used.

You can give your pool a natural appearance and also protect plants by constructing a masonry wall flush with the side of the pool (see page 33). Consult your pool contractor before removing the coping and decking; most city or county building regulations require a 4-foot-wide, solidly paved deck around pools built in expansive soils.

For healthy plants, it is important to have adequate drainage of the pool area. The splash from the pool, rain, and hose water used to clean off paved areas drain away from the pool toward lawns, ground covers, or planting beds. Consequently, the first foot or two adjacent to paved areas often receives too much water. Four methods of overcoming this are shown in the drawings on page 35.

The expanse of water in a pool produces high humidity, especially if the pool is heated, so plants susceptible to mildew are likely to be affected (for example, euonymus and certain roses). In new selections, choose plants whose foliage will withstand moisture.

For areas close to the pool choose plants which drop a minimum of leaves, fruit, resin, and other debris, and which do not attract bees.

Trees and shrubs

If your pool site is surrounded with conifers, evergreen oaks, or eucalyptus, you might consider a screened enclosure for the entire pool and deck area to keep out falling leaves. Whenever possible keep trees away from the pool altogether. Some pool owners who like the effect of trees, however, plant deciduous kinds, preferring a big leaf drop once a year to the small but continuous leaf drop of many evergreens. Fruiting shrubs and trees should be placed completely away from the decking around the pool. The dropping fruit is likely to stain paving, is slippery, and attracts bees, yellow jackets, and ants. Shrubs with thorns or barbs should be placed well away from the bathing area.

Know how much spread a tree's root system is likely to have, so the roots won't interfere with the piping.

ROCK-RIMMED pool simulates a mountain lake, with Canary Island pines providing strong vertical contrast to ground covers of fountain grass, dwarf coyote bush, juniper, wire vine, and rosemary.

RAISED TERRACE near house was formed from dirt excavated for pool. Foreground fishpond is separated from pool by concrete bond beam under slate slab bridge. Juniper, mondo grass, and azaleas dominate the planting.

PLANTING BESIDE THE POOL

Eliminating the decking along one side and planting almost to the water's edge can prevent a harsh effect around a pool. The plants give the pool a natural appearance and integrate it with the rest of the landscaping. A masonry wall, built flush with the side of the pool, separates the planting area from the pool and keeps plants out of the range of most of the splashed water.

In most cases it is not difficult to add this kind of planting bed to your present pool, following the details shown in the drawing below at left. You should consult a pool contractor or landscape architect, however, before removing coping and decking. (Most city or county building departments require a 4-foot-wide, solidly paved deck around pools built in expansive clay soil.)

If you are planning a new pool, you may want to include one or more of these planting beds.

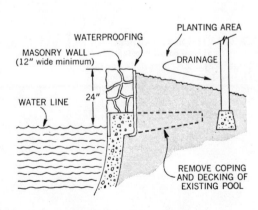

TUBBED PLANTS can add color where planting beds are narrow or no room exists for raised planters. If plants are easily damaged by chemically treated water, they can be moved during times of heavy pool activity.

BRICK PLANTER near pool deck gives vertical line to otherwise flat pool landscape. Circular beds contain Dutch iris. Flat top is good place to display container plants. Electrical outlet at end of planter is useful for entertaining.

GRAVELED STRIP protects a dichondra lawn from pool water. The gravel is contained with 1-inch boards, covered with ½-inch-mesh galvanized hardware cloth stapled to wood. Landscape architect: Courtland Paul.

INSTALLING A DRAINAGE CHANNEL

A drainage channel can be installed to keep water splashed onto the deck from damaging the lawn or running onto the patio. These drawings show four variations of a plan for a gravel-filled drain ditch.

Plan A—Redwood with drain holes covers the gravel drain ditch. To eliminate splinters, use surfaced redwood and sand the edges of the drain holes.

Plan B—To provide drainage where two paved areas join, bricks are set flush with the paving. The size of

the bricks determines the width of the drainage channel.

Plan C—The gravel-filled ditch receives water from the pool deck and drains a raised planter. The redwood header may be capped to make a bench.

Plan D—A redwood header board stops water splashed from the pool and keeps planting bed dirt from washing onto the deck. The deck should slope at least ¼ inch per foot.

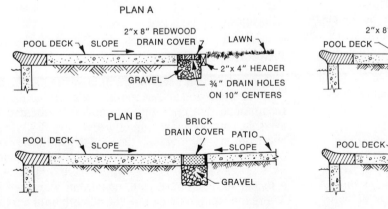

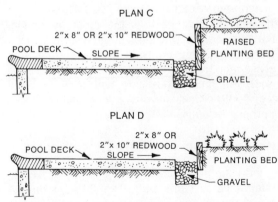

PARTY HOUSE at poolside has dressing rooms, showers, lavatory, small refrigerator and electrical outlets for cooking appliances, and ample room for pool heater, filter, and miscellaneous storage. Designer: John S. O'Brien.

POOLSIDE STRUCTURES AND FENCES

Playing important parts in your pool area are the structures needed to hide equipment, provide storage, filter the sun, block the wind, and otherwise make swimmers and sunbathers comfortable.

Although the pool itself is the main attraction, most of a swimmer's time is spent outside the water—sunbathing, enjoying poolside games, eating, and otherwise relaxing. The more people there are to use the pool, the more likely you will wish to build dressing facilities and showers, a large shaded patio, and perhaps a sauna.

SHELTERS FOR POOLSIDE EQUIPMENT

Along with the pool comes the necessary operating and maintenance equipment. The filter assembly, pump and motor, and heater (if you have one) are best sheltered. In addition, you will need storage space for a vacuum, leaf skimmer, brushes, long handles, and chemicals. Poolside furniture, toys, and other paraphernalia will need to be stored during the winter months but be easily accessible for off-season entertaining.

Protecting the filter

Two requisites for sheltering a filter system are overhead covering and access room. Engineers no longer recommend that operating equipment be located in a pit, because of inaccessibility and danger of damage from standing water. Usually the units are set on a concrete slab at the closest convenient place near the pool. Most home owners have a spot near a fence, garage, house wall, or garden work center where the equipment can be placed with only a minimum structure for shelter.

The most common shelter is a simple wind screen or fence extension with a lean-to roof for water drainage. One or two sides of the shelter should be open for adequate ventilation and easy access to check and backwash the equipment. For the roof, plastic or any other waterproof, easy-to-maintain material can be used. You can match the property fence design and repeat colors in the pool trim to integrate the shelter with the landscaping.

Not all pool equipment is completely waterproof. In most cases, pumps and motors are more water-resistant than waterproof, and adequate shelter is good insurance for best operation and longest life.

Tools and miscellaneous equipment

For long-handled cleaning equipment, open storage is usually the most practical. Hooks and metal eyes in a wall or fence will support brushes, vacuum hose, and skimmer. A cool, dark place is best for chemicals — preferably elsewhere than the filter shelter and locked for safety (see page 73 for information about storing and handling chemicals).

Patio furniture and play equipment are generally stored in the garage, attic, or utility area. Loading them into the filter shelter may obstruct access to the pool equipment. If available and adequately enclosed, a dressing room or built-in seating can provide storage.

During the swimming season, continual exposure of patio furniture to the sun can fade or damage fabric. Cushions will retain their bright colors if they are slip-covered and stored when not in use. Boxes can be designed for quick storage and removal of cushions and also other equipment that is used at poolside.

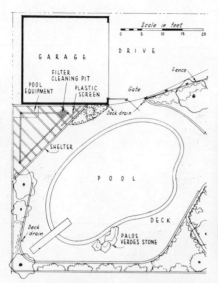

CORNER sun shelter covers lounging area, storage space for pool equipment behind screens. Shelter is 9 feet high, 24 feet long on pool side.

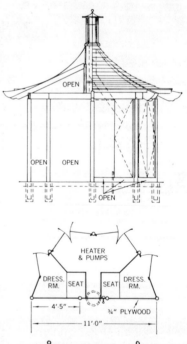

GAZEBO overlooking pool houses pool equipment and dressing rooms, also provides a small semicircle of shade for warm afternoons. The octagonal structure is only 11 feet in diameter. Architect: Morgan Stedman.

SMALL BENCH combines seating with shelter for pump and motor. Waterproof plywood bench has one open side so equipment can be reached for servicing. Valves and pipes are hidden by bench.

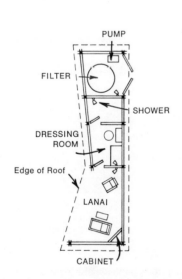

PUMP

FILTER

SHOWER

DRESSING ROOM

Edge of Roof

LANAI

CABINET

COMPACT open-air shelter includes a small lanai for outdoor furniture, a dressing room, a shower, and space for the filter. Chemicals and first aid equipment are kept locked in storage cabinet in lanai. Designer: Gene Loose.

RELAXING OUT OF THE POOL

Built-in seating, inviting spots of shade, and areas protected from the wind create ideal conditions for relaxing or entertaining.

In almost all poolside groups there are bound to be some people who prefer conversation to swimming. Plan for some benches or lounges far enough from the splash zone to ensure a dry and relatively quiet retreat. Patio furniture can dress up the pool and give you a flexible seating arrangement. With a series of pipe inserts in the deck, umbrellas can be arranged in many combinations to add color and provide sun control.

House wings and fencing may provide sufficient shade, though they may cast a shadow over the water if too near the pool. Many pool designers prefer to build a separate shelter to cover only a portion of the deck in the hottest part of late afternoon.

The sun shield can be a simple roof or a large cabana — with dressing rooms, play areas, and storage facilities. A cabana soon becomes the headquarters for poolside activities. As such, it might include cooking and eating facilities and other entertaining features. In more elaborate cases, it might double as a guest house.

Dressing facilities

Even if an outside door leads directly into dressing areas and bathrooms in the house, outside dressing facilities may be desirable; they keep indoor traffic to a minimum and prevent damage to carpets and furniture by wet bathers and swim suits.

The usual requirements for dressing-room structures are privacy, good drainage, a place to sit that will withstand water and dry readily, and ample arrangements for hanging clothes. Other conveniences such as a towel rack and a heater can also be included. Dressing rooms require no roof and can be of simple panel construction. Some pool owners have been able to include dressing facilities in a storage shed or in one section of the garage.

A shower should be included in the arrangement. It need not be any more than an outside fixture located where water will drain easily. Hot water isn't absolutely necessary, but it encourages use of the shower for cleaning feet before entering the pool and washing off chlorinated water after a swim.

SUNBATHERS can stretch out on this generous poolside platform, or you can set up a couple of chairs on it. Designer: George T. Kammerer.

REINFORCED CONCRETE bench was cast in place, needs only occasional hosing for maintenance. Wood sunning bench is 3 by 12 feet. Designers: Warren E. Lauesen (left), John Michael Associates (right).

ENTERTAINING and sunning platform near pool pictured on page 21 has lounging pads, small corner tables, and a gas-fed firepit. Low wall around part of platform serves as backrest. A low table is set over firepit for serving food.

TWO-COMPARTMENT portable
changing room is five 3-foot-wide
louvered doors fastened together.
Lightweight and easy to set up, the
structure can be assembled several
ways as shown in drawings. Doors are
connected at each joint with four
3/8-inch-diameter galvanized lag screws
with washers; curtain rods are
wood closet poles.

DRYING TREE near pool is made of a 3-inch dowel with 1-inch dowels attached horizontally for hanging wet suits and towels.

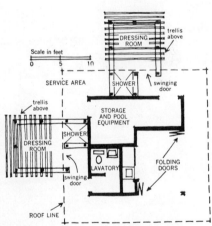

TRELLIS-COVERED dressing room dries fast, is easy to sweep or hose off, has built-in bench and pegs for hanging clothes. See photo on page 36 for exterior view of structure.

OUTDOOR SHOWER drains through spaced deck boards. Dressing rooms are immediately adjacent. Vertical panels are corrugated plastic, the overhead slats redwood. Design architects: Smith and Williams.

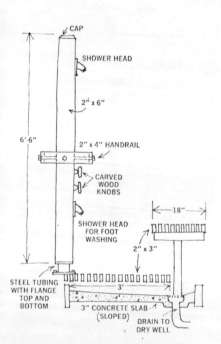

SWIMMER'S shower and foot wash has bench so you can wash feet in comfort. Wooden grid keeps sand from being picked up again when you put your feet down. Handrail around shower also is used as towel rack. Designers: Belt, Collins & Associates.

A sauna

The Finnish sauna and the American swimming pool are perfectly matched. To take full advantage of the cleansing and restorative powers of the dry-heat sauna, it should be followed by a sudden cooling of the body. The Finns roll in a snowbank, but you can go directly from the sauna into your swimming pool with almost the same results. The temperature of the pool water makes little difference; anything will feel cold after the 140° to 240° heat of the sauna.

A home sauna can be installed in a separate build-ing. But if added to the house, the sauna can be used the year around with a shower substituting for the pool in winter. Package kits, complete with stove and heating rocks, are available for home craftsmen, and many plans for larger installations are available.

A sauna needn't be elaborate or even large. The smallest can fit into a space 5 by 8 feet with a 7-foot ceiling. There are no strict requirements on location, but try to keep it as close as possible to the pool, so users can go from hot to cold with a minimum of inconvenience.

INTERLOCKING redwood "bricks" fit within precut framework of this prefabricated sauna. Other woods used for saunas are pine, cedar.

SAUNA INTERIOR has benches at two levels; you start out on the lower level, then move up to lie on the hotter upper bench. This sauna is part of the pavilion pictured on page 24.

POOL FENCES

Most swimming pools are enclosed by a fence of some kind, primarily as a safety feature but also to guarantee privacy. Some cities require non-climbable fences around every pool. Even where they are not required, pool owners should build them as a matter of caution.

You'll never be able to make a pool completely childproof. Toddlers are usually held at bay by a 4½-foot fence, as long as the gate latch is out of reach. But even a fence 5 or 6 feet high may not hold out teenagers determined to go for a swim. Metal mesh should be narrow enough that a child cannot get a toe-hold; there should be no horizontal fence stringers or supports that can be climbed like a ladder.

Where to put the fence depends on your property development and family needs. If you have a fence on your property line, you might surround the immediate pool area with a second, lower fence. The most satisfactory of these fences provides an adequate barrier, yet can be removed easily for swimming and poolside activities.

Safety fences can also double as wind screens and barriers to stop debris from blowing into the water. But solid fences should be avoided; being able to see the pool is a vital precaution against accidents.

HANDSOME baffle screens used with plantings give privacy as well as shelter pool area from wind.

WROUGHT-IRON fence keeps child safely within play area on terrace yet doesn't impair view. Fence sections can be lifted out of sleeves set in concrete to open pool area for entertaining. Landscape architects: Armstrong & Sharfman.

PINE SAPLINGS wired together in panels make a high safety fence around pool and create open-air changing rooms. Panels come in several sizes. Landscape architects: Armstrong & Sharfman.

FREE-STANDING picket fence woven on wire hides pool filter, creates sun pocket. Although fully hidden from pool area, filter is easily reached when servicing is needed. Designer: Margaret Sullivan.

HINGED PANELS roll back and fold against inside of fixed panels on each side. To close off pool area, lock bolts are set at base of each hinged panel. One section can stay loose as gate. Landscape architect: Robert Babcock.

GATE SECTIONS of metal chain link mounted on steep pipe frames and painted black fence this pool when no one is there to "lifeguard." At other times the gates are swung back to leave a 24-foot-wide opening. Landscape architect: W. B. Covert.

ENCLOSED on all sides and partially roofed, this patio is practically free of wind and has pleasant balance of sun and shade. Overhead is of corrugated plastic over steel and wood beams. Designer: Georg Hoy.

POOL ENCLOSURES WITH AN OPEN FEELING

You can enclose your pool completely and still keep an open feeling to the area. These drawings show three different ways to do this, using mesh or panels of glass or plastic as part of the fence.

The pool enclosure at left has a mesh "window" that lets swimmers look past the fence. Shrubs and a built-in bench hide the hard, straight lines of the fence, and a sliding gate gives wide access.

In the center drawing, mesh is used in one end

wall and overhead for maximum light and air. The mesh, slats used on the side walls, and tubbed plants give interesting texture to the area.

Glass or plastic panels create see-through walls for the pool at right. The panels at one end can be removed to open the pool to the patio. An irregular deck pattern has been used to break up the boxlike lines of the pool area. All three designs are by Douglas Baylis.

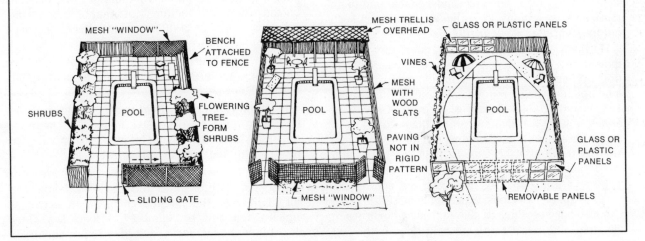

MANUFACTURED 36-foot-wide pool enclosure was mounted on a brick curb to bring eave line to same height as house eave line. Jalousie windows at end were installed by the owner.

ENCLOSED POOLS

Depending on the weather in your locality, swimming in an outdoor pool can be uncomfortable during the spring and fall months, even if the pool is heated, and almost impossible in winter. An enclosed pool may offer a method of extending the swimming season. You can either purchase one of the manufactured canopies, extend your house to include a "pool room," or improvise an enclosure to fit the pool and its surroundings.

In addition to permitting year-around use, the shelter will control summer winds, enable you to do more night swimming, lower heating costs, and keep out most insects and debris.

However, having a roof over your pool allows moisture to condense, creating "greenhouse" conditions. When the temperature outside begins to drop, a completely sealed room can become quite steamy and uncomfortable. Moreover, because of a lack of circulation, these shelters are difficult to cool. In designing a shelter or including a pool as an extension of the house, be sure to plan for maximum ventilation.

There are a variety of manufactured pool enclosures available. The most economical are air-inflated canopies, one of which doubles as a pool cover when deflated. These structures are held down either by a rim of water that serves as an anchor or by fasteners in the deck. A blower provides the slight pressure necessary to keep the canopy inflated. If the shelter is ever punctured or torn, the constant injection of air should prevent the hut from collapsing suddenly and cause it instead to settle slowly to the surface.

Another type of enclosure is constructed of lightweight metal frames paneled with opaque, translucent, or clear fiberglass-reinforced plastic. Some of these are constructed with roll-back roof and/or side panels to allow summer ventilation. Price depends on the size of the shelter. Most manufacturers recommend a minimum of 3 or 4 feet of enclosed deck area around the water.

Other more permanent enclosures of wood, or masonry combined with wood, are also available, but at higher costs.

Extending your house lines to accommodate a pool is usually the most expensive method of sheltering the area. Costs will depend on your location and the type of wall and roof coverings you use.

Be sure to check building codes before investing in a pool enclosure. Some cities consider them accessory buildings, the inflated canopy type included, which means they are subject to setback laws, land development ordinances, and load requirements.

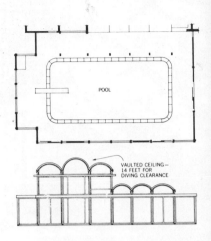

USE OF GLASS opens this structure to the garden and sky. Barrel vaults were used to span a wide area. Drawing shows floor plan and high roof over diving area. Architect: Matt Copenhaver.

FIBERGLASS-reinforced plastic overhead soaks up sun and heat in winter, while sliding doors, large windows, and clerestory vents allow cooling cross ventilation on hot days. Designer: Morgan Stedman.

AIRY PAVILION covers 33 by 60-foot pool deck. Two plywood box beams on steel posts span water; steel tie rods and wood joists, rafters and studs complete framing. Fiberglass screening covers most of structure; translucent sheet plastic over part provides shade. Designers: Gage Brothers.

GLASS-ENCLOSED pool has no off-season. On warm days the glass doors slide open and it seems like the pool is outdoors. For outside view, see photo on page 15.

LIGHTWEIGHT cover for 16 by 46-foot pool is polyethylene sheeting laid over redwood battens bowed crosswise and polypropylene rope run lengthwise. Plastic is replaced every few months.

INFLATABLE shelter retains water heat so swimmers can enjoy the pool during cold winter. When deflated it serves as pool cover to cut down on maintenance chores.

POOL AREA planned with entertaining in mind has wide deck for serving poolside meals and refreshments. A sink and small refrigerator have been installed close at hand. Architect: Richard Bliss Nelson.

LIVING WITH YOUR POOL

After the pool is installed, you will gradually become aware of the many rewards and occasional trials of being a pool owner. If you are prepared, you can make the adjustment smooth and pleasant. This chapter discusses some of the questions to consider concerning pool policy and offers suggestions which have proved successful with other pool owners.

SOME BASIC RULES

Families often find that a new pool becomes the recreation center of the neighborhood. This turn of events may both please and bewilder the pool owners, who are probably quite willing to share their new possession but don't quite know how to go about it.

At first most pool owners hold open house for anyone, anytime, and bear up under the load. Then, after realizing that this greatly limits their own privacy and enjoyment of the pool, they may impose a strict set of rules on everyone. Finally they soften a bit and find the pattern of pool use that fits their lives best, opening the pool to neighbors by invitation and according to the rules of the house.

After the first few months of use, you will discover what rules you need to set up for the use of your pool. To start with, here are some regulations other pool owners have found necessary:

• A weekly schedule, specifying days neighbors are welcome and days they are not even to ask, will ensure your privacy. Many pool owners also set up

certain hours for the younger children, reserving early evening and weekends for adult relaxation.

• All refreshments should be kept completely away from the pool. This applies to adults as well as children. Stray bits of food create a cleanup problem. Moreover, a single broken glass or bottle may cover the floor of the pool with dangerous fragments — and glass is most difficult to see and clean up.

• You may curb dressing-room confusion and unnecessary tracking through the house by requesting neighbors to arrive in their bathing suits, with their own towels and bathing caps. Make a quick check of dressing rooms before guests leave to make sure nothing has been left behind.

• Inflated inner tubes, air mattresses, and similar paraphernalia are enjoyable pool accessories but can be misused. Children in particular can find ways of using these items that are either unsafe to themselves or potentially harmful to the equipment. Some pool owners prohibit all types of accessories, while others just discourage neighborhood children from bringing them into the pool.

• Neighbors who use the pool regularly are usually not hesitant about helping with cleaning chores. Such participation will also make it readily apparent just why bobby pins should not be allowed in the water; why swimmers coated with suntan oil should shower before going into the pool; and why long hair needs to be contained in a bathing cap. A pool without these contaminants is easier to keep clean and much more pleasant to use.

LIGHTING AND POOLSIDE HEATING

Lights and poolside heating help you achieve minimum utilization of your pool by letting you enjoy it at night and during cool weather.

Lighting for effect

A pool takes on some of its greatest appeal after dark, for a swimming party or as a background for patio entertaining. Underwater lights, floods from concealed sources, and special lights around plants and other garden features can create dramatic effects, in addition to lighting the deck area. By turning off the underwater lights, you can transform the pool into a reflecting surface which acts as a mirror for lighted plantings.

Insects attracted by outdoor lighting are not only a distracting nuisance but can quickly litter the pool's surface. In electric lighting, white and blue lamps have the greatest insect attraction and yellow tints the least, with reds in between. Gas lights, which attract fewer insects than most incandescent bulbs, are being used with some success. Only a simple hose connection to the line is needed for each light, and the gas line is not as hazardous as outside electric lines. Gas-fed luau torches can be particularly dramatic around the pool.

Poolside heat sources

Swimming on summer nights or during early spring and late fall is generally possible if your pool is heated and you live in an area with a very mild climate. But unless you expect to make a spirited dash from pool to house between dips, some thought should be given to poolside heating.

An outdoor firepit or barbecue makes a cheery heater for chilly swimmers. Fires can be kindled easily and safely; they provide warmth and also create an attractive lighting effect, particularly if the flames are reflected on the water. (See page 41 for photographs of firepits.)

Portable barbecues and braziers, especially those with open or screened sides, have two advantages: They can be moved almost anywhere to give quick heat, and, if charcoal is burned, they throw very little smoke. A brazier, like an open fireplace, is more efficient if placed near some sort of reflecting surface — wind screens, plantings, or walls.

Radiant heat in the deck is one way to provide general warmth over a large area — if you don't expect too much from it. The tubing takes a long time to warm up, and the slow heat will do little good on cold, windy nights.

PLANTINGS are silhouetted on lighted plastic panels. In foreground is low fixture in plant bed.

UNDERWATER lights brighten surface of pool at night, while lanterns and house lights illume deck and patio. Low light fixtures can be concealed in shrubbery. Architect: Vladimir Ossipoff.

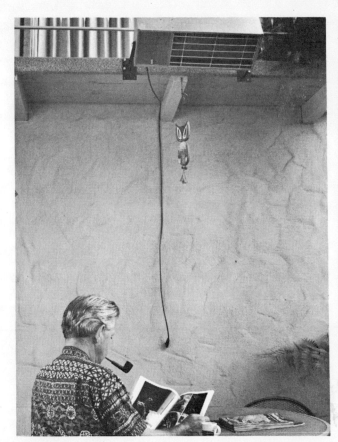

GAS-FIRED infrared heater, left, is mounted to direct heat downward on pool area or patio, is turned on and off by switch on dropcord. Metal basket, right, holds charcoal to serve as poolside warmer.

SNACK BAR can be opened up
by folding back shutters, closed
when not in use. Portable barbecues
are set on counter for cooking.
Architect: Venice Howell.

ENTERTAINING AT THE POOL

A pool is a natural focus for entertaining plans. You will want to give some thought to arrangements for eating and perhaps to organized games.

Poolside refreshments

There's nothing like a quick dip in the pool to encourage ravenous appetites. Cooking is easy on a patio barbecue or fireplace, but some special attention should be given to facilities for eating.

Keep the diners well away from the pool. This keeps debris out of the water and allows for relaxed eating without the threat of splashes. A 15-foot deck width between the pool and the dining table is ideal, but even 10 feet will allow for a little safety zone. Separation with screens and plantings also helps isolate the dining area from the pool.

Many pool owners have found the ideal arrangement to be a two-way counter that permits indoor serving and outdoor eating.

Games

Poolside games don't have to be complicated; the water itself is enough of an attraction to satisfy most guests. Keep the ages of guests in mind. Boys usually take to vigorous, competitive games like water polo, water basketball, and races. But with a mixed crowd, a game of follow the leader, tetherball, or a pan-pushing race is more likely to get everyone involved. If you have the room, shuffleboard, table tennis, and similar deck activities are popular with both young people and adults.

For small children, you might throw a dozen or so corks into the pool and see how many each child can collect in a given time; or have a balloon race across the width of the pool. Fishing games from the poolside are also a good way to keep the young ones occupied.

MASONRY PALLET with electrical outlets is an eating-lounging center right at the pool's edge. Designers: Armstrong & Sharfman.

BASKETBALL backstop has aluminum frame, hooks over edge of pool.

DOLL HOUSEBOAT is kept afloat by unseen styrene foam panels. Sturdy structure is plywood and redwood with transparent acrylic plastic roof.

SOPHISTICATED pool alarm is self-contained and shockproof, uses 12-volt battery, has small transducer that is hung in pool or buried in pool wall. It emits raucous alarm if child or animal falls in pool but doesn't react to wind-caused waves or sounds such as pump.

HEALTH AND SAFETY AROUND THE POOL

Maintaining health standards and safety procedures in and around a swimming pool is an ever-present concern. There must be safe play areas for children as well as adequate water depth for diving. Well maintained fences, strategic lighting, and a pool cover all enter into pool safety. In landscaping around the pool, avoid plants with thorns or with flowers or fruit which attract bees. Select decking and benches which are splinter-free and relatively comfortable on bare skin and feet. Pool safety and health require a day-to-day awareness of what dangers can arise and how to deal with them.

The pool owner is responsible for setting health and safety standards and having the equipment needed to deal with emergencies. Rules should be posted clearly at the pool and mentioned to guests upon their arrival. A cleansing shower should be mandatory prior to entering the pool, to minimize the introduction of bacteria and dirt; and no one with a cold, earache, cuts that may be infected, or any other ailment should go into the water at all. Your local health department can give further recommendations.

Children may need to be reminded often that running, pushing, and horseplay around the pool are not allowed; only one person may be on the diving board at a time; and non-swimmers must never be in water over their heads. Hourly rest periods of 10 to 15 minutes help to calm excited children, give parents a rest, and check over-fatigue. An alarm clock that sounds clearly might be an effective signal announcing rest periods.

No person should swim alone without an observer nearby; but proper supervision cannot be over-emphasized whenever small children are using the pool. Unless you plan to be in the pool area whenever the neighbors are swimming, you should stipulate that a child bring his own supervisor. Keep in mind, however, that supervision is not adequate unless those watching are capable of handling emergencies — and know how to swim.

Be sure that all extension cords to electrical appliances used around the pool, such as radios and refrigerators, are properly grounded to avoid the possibility of electric shock.

Obtain a set of clear instructions for artificial respiration and periodically review the proper techniques. It is imperative to have a set of instructions posted in the pool area. Although most people have been taught how to administer artificial respiration or have at least read about the latest procedures, these techniques may quickly be forgotten. The Red

WIDE SHELF built into one side of this pool provides place for a mother to sit and play with a small child in very shallow water. Children who can already swim use shelf as submerged play platform. Architect: Haydn H. Phillips.

Cross sheet is waterproof and will withstand weather.

Alarm systems are sometimes used by pool owners who cannot see their pool at all times. Some of these devices have sensing mechanisms that are triggered by an object falling into the water. These systems operate by different methods but share a common disadvantage: Someone has to hit the water before the alarm sounds — when he is already in trouble.

The most sensible and effective precaution against accidents is to teach all members of your family, and others who use the pool regularly, how to swim.

Pool insurance

To prevent accidents, the pool owner should make sure that anyone who comes to his house, both guests and deliverymen, knows that the pool is there. Nevertheless, most families, especially those with children, regard comprehensive personal liability insurance as mandatory. Although a pool owner is usually not liable for an injury to an adult trespasser, he may be liable for injury to children who trespass.

If you already have liability insurance on your property, check with your insurance agent; most companies now include swimming pools under existing policies without extra fees. They do, however, require notification of the new installation on your property.

SAFETY FENCE of wire mesh keeps toddlers away from pool. Older children and adults can step over it.

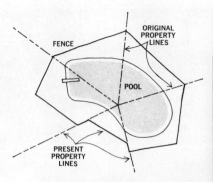

FIVE-FAMILY pool is only a few steps from each of the properties that open to it. Each property owner deeded a corner of land to allow for the curved 20 by 40-foot pool and walk-around deck.

MULTI-FAMILY POOLS

A pool mutually owned by several families offers each family most of the advantages of a private pool and at the same time distributes costs and responsibilities among the owners.

Consult your county department of public health for laws affecting swimming pools. In some states the multi-family pool is regarded as a public rather than a residential pool. Laws regulating public pools are usually much more stringent and may lead to significantly higher installation and maintenance costs. It is advisable to have a general liability insurance policy covering the pool in the name of the association.

The city or county planning commission can provide information on zoning ordinances and city codes. A pool designer should survey the land for rock or water deposits, drainage channels, and power supply.

For safety, and to keep non-swimmers away from the water, the pool and surrounding decking is usually fenced in. Buffer zones between the pool and streets also are good planning features, to ensure privacy and to cut down on dirt and debris blowing into the pool. If the only area available is near a street, fencing or plant screens can be used to isolate the pool.

Obtain the greatest degree of automation of equipment and maintenance systems that you can afford. The pool cost will be somewhat higher, but a pool that takes care of itself will cut down maintenance costs and reduce the need for volunteer "watchmen" and equipment operators.

FIVE-FAMILY POOL

This pool arrangement almost suggested itself, as the lots of five families formed a circle, fitting to-

gether like slices of a pie. Each home has its own private, lockable entrance to the pool area.

The first step was to incorporate. Rules of conduct for the pool were written directly into the corporation bylaws.

An area of about 400 square feet was needed from each of the quarter-acre lots. The five mortgage companies concerned either deeded the required parcel to the corporation at no charge or granted a perpetual easement. The public utility company agreed to vacate its easement on the pool site if the corporation paid for rerouting of underground cables.

From the zoning board the corporation then obtained a special classification to meet health and building codes, since the pool didn't fall into either the private-residential or commercial category.

Total initial cost was $7,500 for the 20 by 40-foot, kidney-shaped pool: $1,500 per family. The first summer's monthly bills for maintenance, chemicals, insurance, and taxes averaged $15 per family.

THREE-FAMILY POOL

This pool serving three families is located on the back portion of one house lot. Before the pool was constructed, a contract was prepared for the proper easements, and the three families are now equal tenants of the pool area.

For initial construction each family invested $1,000 for the basic pool structure. The owners did most of the other work themselves or invested more funds to handle additional expenses as they arose. The owners also do their own maintenance work, so monthly dues of $10 per family are enough to cover taxes, insurance, and cost of chemicals.

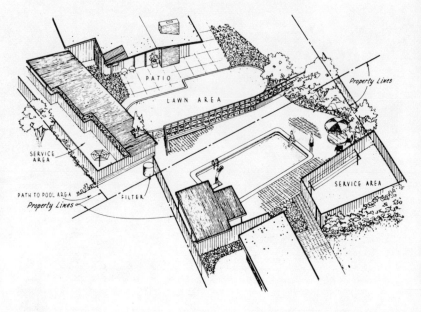

THREE FAMILIES share pool built on back portion of one house lot. Land covered by contract includes all the pool area, a path (left) from one family's lot, and the narrow belt of land in front of the screen on another lot (top).

The contract covering the pool operation includes these key points:

Forfeiture. If one of the contracting families refuses to fulfill financial obligations or abide by the rules for a period of 60 days, the other two members have the right to terminate the defaulting party's right to pool ownership.

Mutual agreement. The contract can be terminated only by agreement of all three parties, who must first agree on disposition of the property and equipment.

Property transfer. If one of the members sells his property, the remaining families can either accept the new neighbors or buy out the departing member's share in the pool and set up a two-family contract.

Insurance. By formal agreement, the owners stipulate that the pool must be covered by accident and liability insurance at all times.

ELEVEN-FAMILY POOL

This pool is situated on a vacant lot in a small subdivision. The subdivision architect drew up the general plans. After a designer had prepared a detailed list of pool specifications, the project was put out on bid and given to a local contractor.

The home owners combined and donated spare time to handle landscaping, fencing, and constructing the bathhouse and storage center. The special abilities of the men in the group came in handy — an electrician did the wiring, a sheet metal man built the shower, a plumber installed the pipes.

Members of the group formed a non-profit corporation, with every adult signing the articles of incorporation. Each family owns one share of stock, and title to the pool and all equipment is held by the corporation. Stockholders invested $600 apiece to cover installation of the pool and materials for auxiliary buildings and fences. The corporation later borrowed $1,500 (through an FHA home improvement loan) from a bank to pay for additional paving around the pool, a lath shelter, and a redwood bench. Each owner was assessed $5 a month, above regular dues, to repay the loan.

Monthly dues of $8 per family cover maintenance costs, including property taxes, insurance, utilities, and twice-a-week servicing by a pool company.

If one member sells his home, the new home owner may purchase pool ownership rights, subject to the approval of the membership. Or the corporation may buy up the share. A board of directors is elected annually, and the officers meet once a month.

Each family has a key to the pool gate, and mothers take turns watching groups of children in the pool. Rules have been established limiting guests to certain days of the week.

ELEVEN-FAMILY pool was installed on a subdivision vacant lot. The home owners formed a corporation, and the title to the pool is held by the corporation.

WHEN SEVERAL families share a pool, each may be able to specify the kind of opening they want from their property to the pool. This gate has mesh-covered viewing hole so small children can watch the activities.

REGULAR use of the leaf skimmer to collect debris from the surface and bottom of the pool is part of the procedure for keeping a pool properly maintained.

WATER TREATMENT AND MAINTENANCE

Proper pool maintenance will keep equipment functioning smoothly, the pool shell and plumbing in good condition, and the water clean. Maintenance of your swimming pool begins as soon as you fill it with water and continues the year around for the life of the pool.

Swimming pool maintenance does not require a great deal of backbreaking labor, but rather a regular schedule of routine work. The time required varies with each installation. If you do all the work yourself, you probably can count on spending 4 to 8 hours a week during the summer. Winter chores are far less time consuming and may be practically nonexistent if you cover the pool. Automatic devices for chemical treatment and pool vacuuming have almost become standard equipment. The initial investment is worthwhile not only by allowing more freedom from chores, but also by safeguarding against unintentional neglect.

Don't try to save pennies by skimping on chemicals or filter; this practice will only increase the chances for damage requiring major repair. The best insurance for keeping costs under control is to know the pool's requirements and make an effort to meet them.

In most metropolitan areas there are service companies that will maintain your pool for a fee, ranging from $30 to $80 per month. The rate depends upon the amount of competition in the area, the number of service calls per week, the size of the pool, and the distances the service men must travel. These companies can be hired to do all your pool maintenance or just to take care of the pool while you are gone on vacation; a swimming pool shouldn't be left without care.

Filtration

The filter system is your main line of defense against impurities (see page 102 for information about the elements of the system). During the summer, when the swimming load is heaviest and the most contaminants enter the pool, the filter should be running

most if not all of the time. For water temperatures of 75° or above, a 12-hour filtration period is generally considered the minimum, but 18 to 24 hours is preferable. In the off-season, 6 to 10 hours a day should be sufficient. You should always be able to see the bottom of the pool clearly at its deepest point.

It is better to over-filter when in doubt than run the risk of improper sanitation. Always keep the filter running for at least an hour after adding chemicals to the pool to insure proper dispersal.

Time clock

Perhaps the smallest expenditure you can make for the greatest convenience is a time clock for the filter system. The clock automatically turns the filter (and heater, if you have one) on and off, regulating cycles accurately and holding power and heating bills to a minimum. Some time clocks turn the heater off shortly before the filter stops, so hot water won't accumulate in the piping.

A time clock can either be installed when the electrical hookup is made for the filter or added later.

FILLING A NEW POOL

Don't be surprised if your new pool looks cloudy after the first filling. The suspended particles present in all drinking water are simply more evident in large quantities of water, but a day or two of filtration along with chlorination will remove the cloudiness. Most pool companies and contractors follow through on both filling and initial water treatment of the pool.

Vinyl-lined and fiberglass pools, depending on the construction methods, are usually filled at the same time as the pool shell is backfilled. Because inlets and skimmer openings must be cut in vinyl liners as the water reaches each level of opening, filling the pool is intermittent. Other types of pools are filled continuously until the water line is reached.

A new plaster pool requires special attention during the first few weeks. It is important to fill it immediately and maintain a continuous flow to prevent dirt rings from forming. Your contractor or plasterer will tell you when to begin filling and how to keep the stream of fresh water from gouging the finish.

It is also necessary to keep dirt from collecting on the walls while the plaster is curing. Frequent brushing will help clean the dirt off, but do not use a vacuum cleaner during the first two weeks — the wheels can mar the surface. A fine, cloudy sediment of plaster dust will result from the brushing, but the filter system will take care of most of the cloudiness; you can scoop out leaves and debris with a leaf skimmer (be careful not to mar the plaster). Do not let the pH fall below 7.4 — acid water is very damaging to new plaster. You can start adding regular doses of chlorine as soon as the pool is full, but don't superchlorinate for about two weeks.

The presence of iron

In some areas, water used to fill the pool may contain iron. Iron causes a red tint, sometimes deepening to a dark brown. Water containing iron should be treated as soon as the pool is filled; otherwise it can stain a plaster pool and clog the filter system.

If your water supply is from a municipal water company such a condition is not likely, but if your source is an underground well not previously treated, test a sample before filling the pool. Fill a glass gallon jug with water from the source and add about ½ ounce liquid or dry chlorine, shake, and let stand for an hour. If the water darkens, you have iron or manganese in the source water.

If the iron content is extensive and you have a plaster pool, seek advice from your pool contractor or a service company; removing iron without staining the plaster can be complex.

Chlorine will oxidize iron and precipitate it out of the solution into rust particles. If you add chlorine to the water to remove the iron, use only small amounts at a time. With each addition, some of the iron particles will settle to the bottom of the pool and should be vacuumed immediately. Repeat the process until the pool water is clear.

Another method is to "floc" the pool with alum. (When alum is dissolved in pool water, a form of aluminum hydroxide — called floc — is formed.) With a sand filter you can floc the water with 1 pound of potassium alum per 5000 gallons of water. (Before adding the alum be sure the pH is in the range of 7.6 to 8.0.) The gel-like floc traps the iron, preventing it from contacting the plaster. Diatomaceous earth filters will collect finer particles than sand, so continuous operation of the system for about 48 hours should clear the pool water. Alum can block diatomaceous earth, so if you use it, the settled floc should be vacuumed to waste disposal from the pool floor. Otherwise it will necessitate frequent changing of the diatomaceous earth.

THE BASICS OF WATER TREATMENT

It is not difficult to keep a swimming pool clear and sanitary. Only a few test kits, chemicals, and a minimum of cleaning equipment are actually needed, though you will find a number of maintenance aids on the market.

The greatest hazards in water maintenance are neglect and over-use of chemicals. Pool care must be consistent; do not experiment with unproven chemicals or techniques, and do not assume that your neighbor's methods will necessarily apply to your pool — each pool is different.

Test kits

Proper water testing is your major guarantee against the development of serious problems. Consider test kits a guide to the well-being of your pool; they provide the information necessary to determine the chemical requirements of the water.

TEST SOLUTION is added to tube filled with pool water to determine the water's chemical requirements.

The basic tests for pH and disinfectant residual are available in a single kit ($2 to $10). Kits that combine pH, disinfectant, alkalinity, acid demand, and hardness tests are available in one convenient unit (about $5 to $13). Cyanuric acid conditioner test kits are usually separate ($7). Check to be sure the kit you buy fits the sanitizing agent you are using; chlorine test kits should never be used for any other chemical, such as bromine or iodine.

Testing is a simple process of filling a small tube with pool water and adding a few drops of test solution. The treated water is then either compared to color standards or calculations provided with the kit. The best time to test the water is in the early evening. Avoid surface water when you fill the tube; take a sample from a depth of at least 12 inches. When you add the specified amount of chemical, mix gently, and don't place your thumb over the top of the tube — body acid can affect the reading. Look at the color against a light (preferably white) background — but not against the sun — and read the test within about 10 seconds after adding the reagent.

Always rinse the tube after use, and never use it for any other type of solution.

WATER BALANCE

Temperature, acidity and alkalinity, and the amount of mineral salts in the water must be kept in balance to prevent corrosion of metal parts, scale deposits, and etching of plaster surfaces. Proper balance also helps to reduce the requirement for sanitizing agents, allowing these chemicals to do their work more effectively.

All water has an acid-alkaline "balance" which is measured on a pH scale. The scale runs from 0 to 14 with the center, 7, indicating a neutral state. Numbers above 7 represent varying degrees of alkalinity, while lower values stand for degrees of acidity. For example, muriatic acid has a pH of about 0, vinegar is 3, distilled water is 7, and lye solutions are close to 14.

Controlling the balance of pool water is vital. The ideal range is slightly on the alkaline side, between

---

SWIMMING POOL VOCABULARY

As a swimming pool owner you will need to learn a specialized vocabulary. The following list of terms and definitions is presented as a guide for the new pool owner who may yet be unfamiliar with swimming pool jargon.

Basically, there are two phases of water treatment: maintaining the balance and disinfecting. Water balance concerns the interaction of temperature, pH, hardness, and total alkalinity of pool water. A "balanced pool" generally means a pool in which scale-causing factors are in correct relation so that scale will not form or dissolve.

- **pH**—The acidity or alkalinity balance of pool water. All water is acidic, neutral, or alkaline.

- **Total alkalinity**—Actual amount of alkali salts present in pool water.

- **Acid demand**—The amount of acid required to lower the pH and total alkalinity of pool water to the correct level.

- **Hardness**—The presence of dissolved mineral solids such as calcium and magnesium salts.

- **Scale**—A crustlike deposit of mineral salts on heating coils and pool surfaces.

Disinfecting the pool refers to keeping the pool water in a sanitary state for swimmers.

- **Bacteria**—Microscopic single-celled organisms not always conducive to a healthful pool; some may carry diseases.

- **Residual**—The amount of disinfectant in the water. Although bromine and iodine are discussed in this book, chlorine is the most widely used disinfectant. For this reason, and to prevent confusion of terms, references to disinfectants will concern chlorine unless otherwise stated.

- **Superchlorination**—An occasional "shock treatment" of pool water by adding 3.5 to 5 ppm of chlorine.

- **Conditioned water**—Generally used in association with an initial conditioning of the water with cyanuric acid.

Other terms that may prove helpful:

- **Algae**—Minute plants that grow in water.

- **Bathing load**—Number of people using pool in a given period.

- **Floc**—A form of aluminum hydroxide produced when alum is dissolved in pool water. It is used as a filter aid with sand filters and traps particles suspended in the water.

- **ppm**—Parts per million (in a pool, the parts of a chemical or mineral per million parts of water, by weight).

- **Test kit**—A packaged supply of testing solutions with comparative color charts and calculations for determining water balance and amount of various chemicals present in pool water.

LIQUID CHLORINE may be poured into pool directly from bottle but must be handled carefully to keep it from splashing.

7.4 and 7.6 on the pH scale. If pH is too high (alkaline), disinfectants are less effective in destroying bacteria and algae; the water will be cloudy, scale can develop on heater coils and plaster surfaces, and the filter can be blocked. If the pH is too low (acid), it will cause eye and skin irritation, corrosion of metal parts, etching and discoloration of plaster. Because over-acidity can be the most serious, the pH should not be allowed to get below 7.2.

Correcting pH is not difficult. The water sample in the test kit will change color according to pH. For example, a phenol red indicator will turn the sample yellow for acid, orange for little or no alkali, and red for high alkalinity. A good test kit should have at least four color gradations between 7.2 and 8.0 so you can get an accurate reading.

During the summer months, pH should be tested about twice a week. In winter, after initial water balance, once a week or even less should be sufficient. Always test for pH after a storm or at other times when large quantities of contaminants have been carried into the water.

Total alkalinity and pH

Although pH and total alkalinity are related, pH is a temporary balance between the acidity and alkalinity of water, while total alkalinity refers to the amount and type (in ppm—parts per million parts of water by weight) of all the alkali soluble salts in the water. To change the level and type of alkali salts, you must change the amount.

The water used in many pools is high in alkalinity, creating problems in adjusting pH. Though pH is quickly controlled by chemicals, it can bounce around on the scale daily or even hourly; this fluctuation can be considerably lessened by adjusting the total alkalinity to within an 80 to 100 ppm range.

Total alkalinity can be very different in different pools because of varying programs of water treatment, water sources, and the amount of fresh water added to the pool. If your pool's alkalinity is over 100 ppm and the pH is over 7.8, add enough acid (a little at a time) to bring the pH down to 7.4. The pH will probably rise again, so continue the treatment until the water tests out consistently at 7.4 to 7.6 over a period of a few days. Each time you add acid the amount should be enough to drop the total alkalinity about 6 to 12 ppm.

As the alkalinity level approaches the 80 to 100 range, the pH should be checked often to make sure it does not drop below 7.2 at any time. Once the 80 to 100 level has been reached, the pH will be buffered to a point where further acid control will be minimal.

Total alkalinity is tested with a simple kit much like a pH tester. After the first adjustment of total alkalinity, it only needs to be sampled about once a month. An acid test kit is available to tell you just how much acid to use, but whether you use the test kit or just add acid until your pH tester shows the right balance, it is advisable to add only small amounts at a time for best control. The best place to add acid is the deep end of the pool, about 1½ feet away from the wall and in an area clear of air suction or return lines. If possible, dilute the acid before adding it to the pool.

Chemicals for raising alkalinity. Sodium carbonate (soda ash) is an inexpensive, effective, quick-acting pH adjuster. Half-pound cakes of soda ash can be suspended in pool water and will dissolve in about three to four hours. To use the chemical in granular form, walk around the pool and sprinkle it into the water. It can also be premixed with water; for the average residential pool dissolve one pound in hot water and pour it into the pool as you walk around the perimeter. Wait 30 minutes (with filter operating) and take a pH reading. If necessary, repeat until the pH has reached the proper level.

Sodium bicarbonate (common baking soda) is inexpensive and easy to use, but only half as strong as soda ash. Use as needed to increase total alkalinity and pH. One and a half pounds raises alkalinity 10 ppm for every 10,000 gallons of water.

Chemicals for lowering alkalinity. Muriatic acid (liquid) is the most popular pH and alkalinity adjuster. It stores well, and small amounts can change pH significantly. However, if incorrectly applied it can be very damaging. One pint for every 5000 gallons of water reduces alkalinity quickly. Add no more than one pint at a time, allowing it to mix thoroughly in pool water (approximately 30 minutes to an hour) before adding more acid. Handle carefully to prevent splashing yourself, and wash off any spillage immediately. Do not add through skimmer.

Sodium bisulphate (dry acid) is the most readily available dry acid for pH adjustment. It is easier to store than liquids and is good for small pools that require small quantities. Use by dissolving in water and spreading around pool. Follow instructions on label for proper amounts. It should be premixed with water (always add acid to water, never water to acid). Handle carefully.

DISINFECTING THE POOL WATER

Bacteria are the main cause of unsanitary pool water. These microscopic organisms, some of them harmful, invade pool water by means of carriers — mostly people. Particularly in smaller pools with heavy bathing loads — including children's wading pools — bacterial control cannot be overemphasized.

There are several ways to disinfect water. A number of electronic and chemical systems have been devised, but they have not become popular because of their high initial cost, maintenance requirements, and lack of effectiveness.

Iodine and bromine have met with intermittent success as disinfectants but are used only on a small percentage of residential pools. Chlorine is by far the most popular disinfecting agent. It is available as gas, liquid, powder, and tablet and has proven to be effective and easy-to-use.

The use of chlorine

Chlorine gas is generally restricted to public pools. Contained in a pressure tank, the gas requires special handling and an automatic feeder. Liquid chlorine (sodium hypochlorite), dry chlorine (calcium hypochlorite), and chlorinated isocyanurics are the major types used in residential and smaller commercial swimming pools.

Automatic chlorinators and hypochlorinators of erosion and solution types ($30 to $500) are increasingly used to maintain the proper amount of disinfectant in the water. They are easily installed, either with a new filtering system or at a later date. Operating continuously (during the filtering cycle), chlorinators regulate the amount of chlorine added to the water in accordance with the pool's requirements. As a result, the pool is kept sanitary at all times and may be left unattended for longer periods.

Although an automatic feeder releases the owner from hand-feeding his pool, he should still regularly use his test kit to keep tabs on the sanitary condition and chemical balance of the water.

Chlorine residual

Whenever you put chlorine in pool water, it immediately goes to work killing algae and bacteria, but in the process some of it is destroyed by these same algae and bacteria. The amount of chlorine used up in this manner is the chlorine demand of the water. The amount of disinfectant left in the water is referred to as chlorine residual. This free residual keeps the pool sanitary, and only a small amount is required.

Swimming-pool water also contains ammonia and other compounds of nitrogen, particularly ammonia nitrogen. Chlorine and ammonia combine to form "chlormines" which cause eye burning, skin irritation, and the unpleasant odor often associated with chlorine, particularly pungent if the pH is low. If you can smell the chlorine, there isn't enough free chlorine in the water, as chlorine in an uncombined state is practically odorless. Nitrogenous compounds can be blown by wind into the pool in the form of fertilizers used on nearby lawns or planting areas.

The chlorine residual not combined with nitrogen should never drop below 0.4 ppm; it can range up to 1.0 ppm or even a little higher, but 0.8 ppm is ideal.

Sunlight, bathing load, water temperature, and wind are the major factors affecting depletion of chlorine residual. Sunlight can dissipate the chlorine, and the more people in your pool, the heavier the work load for the chemical.

Regular use of chlorine — three or four times a week during the summer — should keep the residual at a safe level. But a day of heavy use can destroy all the chlorine in the water unless you take preventive measures by adding an extra dose before swimmers arrive. Even then, the supply may have to be replenished at the end of the day to restore the residual to its proper level.

Chlorine residual is tested much the same way as pH. Follow the instructions that are provided with your test kit.

Superchlorination

Superchlorination is an extra treatment applied occasionally to pool water to burn out nitrogen compounds. Bacteria, algae, and ammonia can build up to a point beyond what normal treatment can control, so about every other week three to five times the normal dose of chlorine is added to the pool. Usually liquid chlorine is the form preferred for superchlorination.

Increased algae growth and heavy bathing loads when water temperatures are above 85 degrees may necessitate superchlorination as often as once a week. Every two weeks should be enough for water in the 75 to 85-degree range; colder pools can sometimes do without any extra dosage unless they are heavily used.

Many chemical companies recommend that you superchlorinate after each fertilization of lawn or planting areas near the pool to counteract nitrogen released from fertilizer blown into the pool.

Add any chemicals to your pool in the early morning or preferably late evening; keep the filter system in operation for at least an hour afterwards to ensure proper mixing. Superchlorination should be done only after sundown, since the ultra-violet sun rays are likely to destroy some of the chemical. (See Conditioning the pool, below.) Close the pool to swimmers until the residual level drops to normal.

Conditioning the pool

The major disadvantage of chlorine is its tendency to dissipate in sunlight. Many pool owners use cyanuric acid to filter out ultraviolet sun rays, permitting the chlorine to do its job of disinfecting.

The swimming pool usually is conditioned to about 30 ppm of cyanuric acid when the pool is first filled, and additional application is needed only as splashout and backwashing require water to be added. Although conditioning of the pool requires a special test kit ($5 to $10) and adds to the initial cost of chemicals, expenditure is usually compensated for by the long-term effects on the chlorine residual and reduced need of acid for pH adjustment.

Although referred to as an acid, cyanuric acid has very low toxicity and little effect on pH. According to the U.S. Public Health Service, concentrations of up to 100 ppm are safe; cyanuric acid below that level tends to be self-regulating.

Sanitizing agents

Liquid chlorine (sodium hypochlorite) is an inexpensive, popular chlorine form. It disperses quickly in water and leaves no residue to add to water hardness. It has a very high chlorine content and requires careful handling to avoid splashing, damage to clothes, and possible fading of colors in pool finishes. If stored too long, liquid chlorine has a tendency to deteriorate. Liquid chlorine raises the alkalinity and pH of pool water.

Dry chlorine (calcium hypochlorite) is available in tablet or granulated form. It is inexpensive and stores well but disperses more slowly than liquid chlorine. It contains about 70 per cent available chlorine and is particularly good for spot treatments of clinging algae.

Although the granulated type may be added directly to the pool, it leaves a calcium residue that can clog diatomaceous filters, turn the water milky, and sometimes cause the grains of sand in sand filters to cement. To prevent this, combine 8 ounces of powder with 10 quarts of water in a non-metallic container. Stir for at least 30 seconds, then set aside out of the sun for 30 minutes to allow the solids to settle. Pour the clear liquid into the pool, and discard the sediment.

Tablets are suspended in baskets over the inlet lines in the pool. Chlorine is released gradually as the flow of incoming water dissolves the tablets.

Calcium hypochlorite, like liquid chlorine, raises the alkalinity and pH of the pool water.

Chlorinated isocyanurics are chlorine compounds with cyanuric acid base. After a pool has been initially conditioned with cyanuric acid, this form of chlorine will automatically replace the conditioner lost through splashout and backwash. These chlorine compounds are easy to use, dissolve readily, leave no calcium residue to damage filter media, do not appreciably alter pH, and are available in tablets, sticks, or granulated form.

Continued use of the chlorinated isocyanurics may cause the cyanuric level in the water to gradually increase over a period of years if water is not discarded by backwash, splashout, and so on. If the water tests out at over 100 ppm, the pool may have to be partially drained and refilled with fresh water. To forestall this, liquid chlorine can be used as a superchlorinator instead of the isocyanurics.

Elemental bromine is equal to chlorine as a bactericide, but the extreme care required in handling has limited its use in residential pools. Organic bromine is available in stick form and can be used in the same manner as the hypochlorites and isocyanurics, but it is more costly. The sticks dissolve into the recirculating system from a pressure vessel which controls the rate the disinfectant is fed into the pool water. Elemental bromine lowers the pH, to the acidic side.

Iodine has been used to a limited degree. However, although easy to use, it is less effective than chlorine and can turn the water green. Iodine is difficult to test for residual, and the water balance must be carefully controlled.

SPECIAL WATER PROBLEMS

You probably will have at least one of the following problems from time to time. Some are inherent in the original water supply; others arise because of extreme weather conditions, temporary lapses in chemical treatment or filtration, or heavy bathing loads.

Algae

Following a regular routine of water maintenance normally will keep algae under control, but they sometimes appear anyway. If the water takes on a greenish cast and, in the case of plaster, black or dark green spots appear on the surface finish, you probably have algae.

There are two types of algae: free-floating and clinging. Some of the clinging varieties may resist all of your regular efforts and hang on as black, green, or brown patches on plaster finishes. There are several ways to get rid of an algae infestation.

1. Check the total alkalinity of your pool. If it is not in the 80 to 100 ppm range, adjust it. Also adjust the pH to 7.2 to 7.4, then superchlorinate with as much as 1 gallon of liquid chlorine (or 2 pounds of dry chlorine) for each 10,000 gallons of water. Shut down the filter for about 24 hours. Brush walls briskly, restart filter, and vacuum away dead algae. Do not allow swimmers in the pool during this period.

Persistent colonies clinging to interior surfaces sometimes can be destroyed by pouring liquid chlorine right on top of them, or by placing dry chlorine in a nylon stocking and using it as a scouring pad (wear rubber gloves). However, only the outer layers of cells may be killed, leaving surviving cells beneath to re-emerge when growth conditions are favorable.

2. If algae still remain, there are several effective algaecides on the market. Many pool contractors and service companies recommend that a dose of algaecide be added occasionally as a routine part of maintenance. Make sure the algaecide you select is effective against all strains of algae, and carefully follow instructions on the label. Consult your pool service man for recommendations.

3. Pool stones are available for grinding off spots of algae on plaster. Either dive down to a spot or

---

PROPER USE OF CHEMICALS

Swimming pool maintenance involves chemicals which could be harmful if not handled properly, so it is very important to follow certain procedures in using them.

1. Never use your neighbor's pool water test results or filtration procedures as a guide for your own pool.

2. Never mix any pool chemicals together unless so directed by the manufacturer on the label of the container. Common household bleaches, if used to clean pool areas, must never be mixed with or used simultaneously with household drain cleaners: the combination of chemicals will form poisonous chlorine gas.

3. Keep all pool chemicals and cleaning agents sealed and stored in a locked, dry area out of reach of children; the key should be available only to adults familiar with the use of the chemicals.

4. Do not store chemicals in enclosed filter rooms, since even covered containers can emit corrosive fumes.

5. Add chemicals to water carefully. Hold a liquid container close to surface of water so that it will not splash on skin or clothes; sprinkle granulated products close to water surface so they will not be blown.

6. Wash hands with soap and water after using chemicals.

7. Handle all acids with extreme care. Follow manufacturers' directions carefully. Dilute before adding to pool.

8. Always check labels of chemicals, both when you buy them and when you use them. Labels sometimes look similar; adding the wrong chemical can lead to harmful conditions.

attach the stone to the end of your brush pole and work from above.

4. If algae persists, call in a professional service company for help. There are other, more complex algae treatments available, but it is better to rely on competent advice before adding strange chemicals to the water.

5. Check chlorine residual and pH after heavy chemical treatments, and do not allow swimmers in pool until water is properly balanced and chlorine content is at a safe level.

Colored water

Color in a freshly filled pool may result from algae or vegetation sources such as tannin; the color will bleach out when sufficient chlorine is added. Color also is caused by suspended dirt, which filtration will remove.

The most troublesome causes of coloration are minerals in the water. Many pools will fill perfectly clear but become reddish brown or black after standing exposed to the air, or when chlorine is added. This is caused by a soluble form of iron or manganese which becomes insoluble when oxidized by oxygen or chlorine (see section on iron content, page 68).

Hazy or turbid water is either over-alkaline, needs more filtration or chlorination, or both.

Green, blue-green, or milky water probably is over-acid and low in total alkalinity. If both acid and alkalinity are normal, you may have iron in the fill water.

With any colored water it will be necessary to filter almost continuously and test and adjust the water chemically until the condition is corrected.

HOW TO ESTIMATE A POOL'S GALLON CAPACITY

You should have a record of your pool's gallon capacity, since this measurement often is used to figure amounts of chemicals for treating the water. The following formulas will give you the total gallons your pool will hold.

Estimating capacity by surface area:
- Surface area (sq. ft.) x average depth x 7.5

Estimating capacity by shape:
- Rectangular—Length x width x average depth x 7.5
- Circular — Diameter x diameter x average depth x 5.9
- Oval—Length x width x average depth x 5.9

Stains

A concrete pool can be stained by debris, metal objects, algae, and mineral deposits. Yellow or reddish-brown stains may be caused by iron in the fill water. Too much acid added to the water at one time can cause stains and, if added too close to surface skimmer, will be carried into the pipe and filter systems, causing corrosion particles to appear as stains. It also can corrode the piping, filter, and heating system. Maintain the proper pH to help prevent these problems.

Hairpins, toys, or other metallic objects dropped in the pool should be removed immediately to prevent rust stains.

On a plaster finish, buffing ordinary stains with waterproof sandpaper may remove them. A dilute solution of muriatic acid (1 part acid to 10 parts water) also can be used, if great care is taken not to etch the surrounding plaster. Excess etching not only visually mars the surface, but the cracks and crevices become excellent breeding grounds for algae. On a painted pool, stains can be removed by scrubbing them with a strong detergent or chlorine solution.

Scale

Scale is caused mainly by an accumulation of calcium salts along with high pH and alkalinity. It usually will appear at first on heater coils, so the pool heater should not be operated when the pH is above the 7.6 to 8.0 range. After a winter of disuse, be sure the pH is properly adjusted before using the heater.

Scale also will appear as a gray or brownish crust on tile or cement. Maintaining total alkalinity and hardness levels in balance helps control these deposits; however, evaporation causes most pools to develop increasingly higher mineral contents as the years go by. The water should be checked every year or two by a professional to make sure the mineral level does not get high enough to cause a serious scale problem.

Well developed scale deposits usually cannot be removed with sandpaper or acid solution. The only alternative is to call in a professional to power-sand and acid-wash the pool.

Corrosion and electrolysis

Corrosion can result from an over-acidic condition, improper use of acid chemicals, or oxidation. Corrosion also can be caused by electrolysis. Whenever two different metals come in contact with chemically treated water, a small electrical current flows between the metals. This current does not give an electric "shock," but it can cause corrosion of active metals such as iron and produce rust spots on metal.

FLOATING automatic pool cleaner has hoses that hang close to pool walls and bottom to churn water, forcing dirt into filter and larger debris into the leaf trap.

If copper tanks and pipes in the recirculation system are seriously corroded by electrolysis, the copper must be replaced in a short time. Although many pools are never troubled with electrolysis, it does happen often enough to warrant preventive measures. Periodic checks for corrosion should be made near valves where copper and iron, or other dissimilar metals, come together. In filter tanks, engineers may recommend the use of a sacrificial magnesium anode to draw the electrolytic deposit away from the tank.

Electrolysis can create unsightly blacking of chrome parts. Because the source of the electric current often is evasive, an engineering firm or pool company should diagnose the problem.

WHAT COMES FIRST?

Most pool companies and contractors include initial filling and water treatment in your contract. If you are confronted with the task yourself, the following procedure is recommended.

1. Test source of fill water. Use your test kits for pH and disinfectant, total alkalinity, hardness, and acid demand. This survey of the water's condition will give you a preliminary idea of the type and amount of chemicals needed to balance and disinfect the pool water. Also check for iron content (see page 68).

2. Fill pool according to contractor's instructions.

3. Start filter according to manufacturer's instruc-

tions; add about 2 gallons of liquid chlorine, or the equivalent of dry chlorine. Brush down pool walls to remove sediment and dirt, then test for chlorine again.

4. Adjust total alkalinity to within 80 to 100 ppm, adding acid according to acid demand test kit. Also test for pH and adjust to within 7.4 to 7.6. (Remember — do not mix any chemicals together; allow time for each addition to circulate thoroughly; and do not allow the pH to drop below 7.2.)

5. Condition the pool water with cyanuric acid to 30 ppm.

CLEANING THE POOL

A thorough cleaning once a week and intermittent touch-ups before and after days of heavy use usually will keep the pool clean and attractive.

Maintenance equipment

The basic pieces of equipment required to maintain a residential pool are a vacuum cleaner, brushes, leaf skimmer, and water test kits. A few extra purchases can make maintenance easier, but none are really essential. New items are constantly being developed to reduce the maintenance time — check any equipment manufacturer's catalog.

Vacuum cleaner. There are two types of non-automated vacuum cleaners. The first works from a vacuum inlet that is part of the filter system. It consists

CLEANING equipment and pool accessories hang neatly along a wall near pool. Hangers are made from 16-inch strips of aluminum. Designer: C. B. Hamill.

LONG HANDLE for skimmer stays light and buoyant if a cork is fitted inside lower end to keep pole from filling with water. To sink pole for use with brush, fill partially with pool water (right).

of a suction head, wheels (on most) for mobility, a nylon brush (not included in some models), a floating hose, and a handle. The cleaner is connected to the vacuum fitting, and as you push the cleaner around the bottom of the pool it pulls water, dirt, and debris into the filter system. Leaves and other large objects are caught in the pump strainer; the smaller particles are removed in the filter. Clear water is then returned to the pool through the normal inlets. Cost of this type of vacuum cleaner is $65 to $95, depending on the materials used and the size and type of suction head. Cove angles and pool size determine the type of suction head required.

The second non-automated cleaner does not depend upon the filtration system as its power source. It can, therefore, be used in pools without vacuum fittings. Called a jet cleaner, it is quickly assembled and moves rapidly across the pool surfaces. It uses a garden hose connected to a standard house faucet to create the vacuum action at the cleaner head. The hose should be at least ¾-inch diameter and no more than 50 feet long. There must be at least 40 pounds of water pressure at the hose faucet.

Water is forced through the hose into the throat of the suction head, which in turn creates water flow from the cleaner opening and up into a filter bag attached to the vacuum cleaner. Refuse is caught in the filter bag, while the clean water passes through the weave of the cotton or synthetic cloth bag. When vacuuming is completed, the filter bag is removed and cleaned.

Jet cleaners remove leaves much better than the standard vacuum cleaner and filter combination; on the other hand, the standard combination is more efficient at picking up and retaining fine dirt. Jet units range in price from $20 to $60, including suction head and filter bag.

Automatic pool cleaning systems eliminate the need for a vacuum cleaner and sometimes even brushes. Most systems require that inlets be imbedded in the pool at the time of construction. Clean water coming from the filter is forced through these inlets at high pressure; depending on the type of cleaner, the water is agitated by a system of hoses or hydrojet action. Costs vary according to the type of installation.

A popular portable pool cleaner consists of a mobile floating unit with long hoses that dangle close to the walls and floor. Water is pumped from the filter to the floating unit, via a booster pump that increases pressure, and then out through the hoses. Dirt is churned into suspension to be filtered, while leaves and other large particles are pushed down into a leaf trap over the main drain. The floating unit has enough feeder line to propel it over the entire pool surface, so there are no "dead" spots of uncirculated water. Cost is about $500.

If you select an electrically operated vacuum cleaner, check the manufacturer's instructions carefully. Electrical connections should be made only through a heavy duty, commercial grade three-wire extension cord grounded to a household outlet.

Leaf skimmer. The leaf skimmer is an aluminum, stainless steel, or plastic frame with a plastic mesh skimming net. These units are available in a number of sizes and styles — including one with a scoop surface for removing large objects. A skimmer may cost $5 to $20, without handle.

Brushes. If your pool has paint, vinyl, or fiberglass finish, you need only one brush for general cleaning of walls and floor. Nylon bristles usually are recommended for long life ($10 to $20 without handle). If your pool has a plaster finish, you will also need a stainless steel brush ($8 to $15) for removing algae, rust stains, and entrenched dirt.

Brushes come in many sizes, and some have curved ends for cleaning coved corners.

Handle. Single-piece or telescopic aluminum handles that fit the vacuum cleaner, leaf skimmer, and brushes are available in lengths ranging from 8 to 16 feet ($5 to $10). One handle is enough for most pool owners. Telescopic handles are advantageous when trees or structures close to the water limit maneuverability.

Regular cleaning procedure

Although there is no set pattern for pool clean-up, the National Swimming Pool Institute recommends an eight-step maintenance procedure that is followed by many pool service firms and will serve as a good starting point for new pool owners.

1. Test the water. (See sections on Water Balance and Disinfecting the Pool Water, pages 69 and 71.)

2. Use the leaf skimmer to collect all leaves, pieces of paper, moths, and other debris on the surface of the pool or on the bottom. It is much easier to skim the surface than dredge the bottom, so many pool owners take the time to use the skimmer often —even every day if the wind is blowing—to remove debris before it sinks.

3. Clean the tile and walls. The scum line that forms on waterline tile is a combination of oil and dust, and usually it can be removed with regular household scouring powders and a cleaning rag or sponge. Many companies offer special tile cleaners that are applied with a brush. (Steel wool should never be used to clean tile, because the iron particles can stain plaster.) Light scale deposits can be removed from tile with a soft pumice stone block (available at pool supply houses). In some cases a razor blade may be needed. If heavy scale persists, a serious water problem is indicated; professional help should be called.

TILE TRIM is cleaned with a brush and powdered household cleaner to remove scum that forms at the water line from combined dirt and oil.

A nylon brush normally is tough enough to remove the dirt that clings to pool walls. A stainless steel brush can be used periodically on plaster to dislodge algae and stubborn dirt. Brush the walls all the way down to the floor, so the refuse can be picked up with the vacuum cleaner. Whenever possible brush towards the main drain, and some of the dirt will be pulled into the filter system as you work. Start at the shallow end of the pool and work toward the deep water. Overlap strokes so the entire surface receives a good scrubbing.

4. Clean the skimmer and the hair and leaf strainer in the filter. Make sure all debris is removed to allow maximum suction during the vacuuming.

5. Vacuum the pool. This should be done at least once a week, more often if wind and rain have brought in an extra heavy dose of foreign material. Operating a vacuum cleaner is not a difficult job; with a jet-type unit, assembly of the vacuum involves only hooking up a garden hose and attaching the filter bag. But with a vacuum that is attached to a filter system outlet and uses the filter pump for power, take care to prevent air from being pumped through the lines. Your vacuum cleaner will come with complete operation instructions.

Try not to run fresh water into the pool while vacuuming. Do it beforehand to have the advantage of looking through still water while working. If ripples or the sun's glare prevent you from seeing the bottom clearly, sprinkle powdered tile cleaner or kitchen sink cleaner on the water; you will be able to see right through.

It is sometimes advisable to vacuum directly to waste. This is often recommended if there are heavy precipitates or an unusually high soil load to be removed. Opening the waste lines of the filter will increase the suction and also reduce the load on the filter media. This operation takes water from the pool, so do not let it continue too long.

6. Backwash and service the filter. Regular and thorough backwashing extends the life of equipment.

7. Add chemicals. The type and amount depends on test results, past experience, anticipated use.

8. Hose the coping and deck. Always hose the pool area before swimmers arrive or they will track dust and dirt into the water. Keep the water spray directed away from the pool to prevent silt from being washed into the clean water. During the summer months, it is a good idea to sweep down the decking occasionally with a 5 per cent chlorine solution to kill bacteria and prevent the spread of infection. (Be careful not to let the solution drain onto lawn or plantings.)

NON-AUTOMATED vacuum that works from a vacuum inlet in the filter system includes hose and suction head with handle to guide it.

Storm clean-up

A rain or wind storm can litter your pool with so much debris that it is unfit for swimming. The deck skimmer and filter will handle much of the cleaning job, but if the pool surface is covered with leaves and debris, you probably will need to spend some extra time with your leaf skimmer. Coping and deck areas should be hosed down. Brush the pool walls and follow with a thorough vacuuming. If the vacuum leaves wheel tracks on the sides or bottom, there is still dirt clinging to the plaster. Brush the sides again (filter running), push dirt toward the main drain, and let it settle before making another pass with the vacuum.

An automatic cleaner will keep dirt to a minimum if in operation during a period of high winds and stormy weather.

MAINTENANCE OF MECHANICAL EQUIPMENT

Maintenance of the filter system involves keeping it in working order and watching for small troubles that could develop into costly problems. Check the system in strict accordance with the manufacturer's specifications. When you buy the equipment, detailed operating instructions will be provided. If there are any problems it usually is best to go directly to the manufacturer or pool company that installed the equipment.

Sand filters

Proper water control is the crucial factor for the maintenance of sand filters. Low pH means that acid water is passing through the valves and tank, while a high pH and high level of calcium precipitation can turn the sand bed into a solid mass of scale. But if the water is properly controlled, the filter will need no extra treatment.

Frequent and adequate backwashing of the filter will prevent the filtering media from becoming packed or clogged with dirt, which substantially reduces the filtering surface. For finer filtration in a sand unit, add alum. Alum forms a gelatinous coating over the sand and traps small particles that would otherwise pass through. It should be dissolved and fed slowly into the filter at a rate between $1/10$ and $1/3$ pound per square foot of filter area. When adding alum, be sure the pH of the water is above 7.4; alum will not flocculate in acid conditions.

PUMP STRAINER keeps debris from entering pump. Lid is removed to clean the strainer, then securely replaced to prevent air from entering the pump.

Diatomaceous earth filters

Most important for the maintenance of diatomaceous earth filters is the cleaning of the elements. Follow the manufacturer's specifications carefully for both the cleaning and replacement of the media.

Pressure D. E. filters are usually backwashed by spinning, reversing the flow (as with sand units), or a combination of both methods. If it becomes necessary to backwash with rapidly increasing frequency, the elements have become clogged and the unit must be taken apart to be cleaned by hand. You may want to consult a pool service company for advice.

Pump and motor

The pump and motor should require very little maintenance by the pool owner. The specification sheets that accompany the units will clearly explain what lubrication, if any, is necessary and how often the units will require service. Guard against loss of prime in the pump; if large amounts of air are drawn into the pump it will operate dry, and the seal may be damaged. If the pump loses its prime, stop the motor, fill the hair and lint strainer with water, replace the lid tightly, and start the motor.

The pump strainer keeps leaves and other debris that get into the piping from entering the pump; it should be cleaned before and after vacuuming and before backwashing. When returning the strainer to the pump, be sure it is full of water and that the lid is on tight to prevent an air leak.

Heater

The instruction manual that accompanies the heater will provide detailed maintenance instructions. Heaters, particularly the direct systems, tend to form scale. If the water used in the pool is hard, most manufacturers recommend that the heater be disassembled and inspected once or even twice a year. If scale has formed, the tubes can be cleaned with wire brushes or acid. In extreme cases the tubes may have to be replaced. Most of this trouble can be avoided by buying a well designed heater and keeping the water in chemical balance.

Accessories

The chrome-plated brass, stainless steel, and aluminum used for pool accessories require only minimum care to retain a good appearance. Surfaces out of water can be cleaned and polished with a good chrome cleaner. For underwater sections a household cleaner can be used, if applied carefully to prevent scratches.

Most diving boards are fiberglass, or wood laminated with fiberglass, coated with a non-skid material. Very little maintenance is required for these boards. However, if cracks appear, have them repaired at once. In colder climates diving boards should be stored during winter.

Once a year remove the metal ladder from its moorings. Dry it completely in the sun and scrape away any algae that has formed on hidden surfaces such as the area around the anchor bolts or under the steps.

REPAIRING AND REFINISHING THE POOL

Despite all the steps that can be taken during pool construction to provide the soundest possible structure, some repairs or refinishing eventually may be required.

Leaks in concrete

A certain amount of water loss from a swimming pool can be expected from normal evaporation, splashing, and filter cleaning. But if you notice a steady drop in the waterline, even in cool weather when the pool is rarely used, there may be a leak.

All leaks should be repaired as soon as possible. Water that leaks out could cause serious difficulties either by undermining the pool or deck or by expanding the soil so it exerts enough pressure to crack the pool shell.

The first step in finding a leak is to search the walls just above the water line, if the water has dropped below the tile line. Look around fittings, the light niche, and anchors below water. Examine hairline cracks and discolored sections of the plaster, and check the filter for leakage. You can call in a service company to pressure-test the plumbing to see if there is a break in one of the underground lines.

If you still cannot find the source of the leak there may be a crack deep in the pool, necessitating complete drainage to find it. Draining a pool is not a procedure to be taken lightly; most pool companies and service men recommend that professionals be called in to determine the nature of the leakage and repair it.

Once the leak is repaired, assuming the original construction is sound, you shouldn't have to expect cracking to recur. However, if the pool is badly cracked or has shifted, a new 3 or 4-inch reinforced concrete shell may be necessary. This can either be poured or gunited on the old shell after the surface has been sandblasted and etched.

Refinishing concrete

The original wall surface of a concrete pool may need to be replaced because of natural paint deterioration or the unexpected destruction of plaster caused by improper maintenance, scale formation, acid etching, or algae deposits.

Plaster. A plaster finish may develop small cracks, usually caused by rapid changes in temperature. If the cracks are not causing the pool to leak, they can be filled by forcing a caulking compound into the cracks with a putty knife and smoothing it down.

Algae infestations, stains, or excessive scaling resulting from months of disuse or faulty maintenance are treated either by an acid washing or by sanding.

Acid washing requires draining the pool and washing down the entire surface with an acid solution.

Sanding is the better method. If black algae have penetrated into the plaster and concrete shell, it may be necessary to chip a small portion of the material away and patch the spot. Normal maintenance (brushing the walls) and water action will soon blend it into the surrounding plaster. Refinishing plaster is a job for professionals, though a few amateurs have done the job themselves. If you do tackle it, first get advice from a service man or equipment supplier.

Replastering is an expensive job, but it will erase a multitude of maintenance sins and give a worn pool a sparkling new face. Plaster will not bond with any surface except clean-etched or sandblasted concrete, so replastering must be preceded by a thorough cleaning or sandblasting job.

Paint. If an etched plaster finish shows no signs of chalking, powdering, or flaking, paint can be applied over it. Worn paint may be recoated, but only with the same type of paint used originally (chlorinated rubber will not bond with vinyl, or vice versa). As for any repair work or finish renewal that requires draining the pool, it is recommended that professionals be called in for advice or to do the whole job.

If an earlier coat of paint is in fair shape, small chips and blisters may be buffed away to form a smooth enough surface. The entire pool is then washed thoroughly, and paint is applied according to the manufacturer's specifications. If more than half of the finish has flaked or peeled, all the old paint should be removed with a power sander or by sandblasting — paint removers are not recommended, since they leave a waxlike residue. If 25 to 50 per cent of the finish is bad a rotary scraper may be used to shave off old paint a layer at a time to prepare the surface, although you take a calculated risk in not removing the old paint entirely.

If paint has peeled off the wall in large sections, you probably have a moisture problem; liquids trapped under the coat may have pushed the paint off from behind. A pool service company can suggest the proper remedy.

Vinyl liners

Repairing a tear or leak in a vinyl liner actually is a simple task. The material will bond readily with a vinyl patch to form a watertight seal.

Kits are available for patching liners; some vinyl companies offer underwater patching kits, so there is no need to drain the pool to make repairs. If a kit is not available, a patch can be applied in the following manner:

1. Purchase from the manufacturer a sheet of vinyl that matches the pool. Cut it to adequately cover the tear.

2. Clean the surface of the liner carefully with a household cleaner to be sure there are no chemicals or dirt on the material, and smooth the edges of the torn section.

3. Prepare a "glue" by mixing a vinyl solvent (acetone or methyl ethyl ketone) and a small piece of the vinyl material. Paint both the wall surface and the patch with this glue, apply the patch to the pool wall, and smooth it firmly in place.

The patch will be equal in strength to the regular pool wall; the solvent causes the two pieces of vinyl to dissolve and then reharden as a single element. The repair isn't even a "patch" but rather a fusion of materials.

While the actual life span of a vinyl liner is not known, manufacturers will guarantee it for 10 years. Eventually, a liner will deteriorate sufficiently to necessitate replacement.

Most liners are installed with special fittings that facilitate the removal of the old unit and the installation of the new one. However, the old liner must be removed carefully and the new liner cut exactly to fit the existing pool size and shape. The procedure for replacement is the same as that for initial installation (see page 95). While the liner is out of the pool, check the pool walls and floor to be sure no structural difficulties have arisen. The sand bed may need reconditioning, more sand, or repacking. Make sure wall joints — particularly if your pool has wood walls — are solid and show no evidence of damage or deterioration. Concrete block walls may require a new plaster coat if the old surface has become marred or rough. Do not be concerned if the walls leak slightly; since the liner is the waterproofing element, the structure should be solid but not necessarily watertight.

Steel pools

Under normal conditions, steel-walled pools (1/4-inch plate with welded seams) not porcelainized only require repainting for correct maintenance. Rust indicates either that the paint was improperly applied or that a touch-up coat is needed. Check small rust spots immediately to prevent spreading.

Fiberglass pools

If a leak occurs in a fiberglass one-piece shell the pool must be drained down to the crack and the material relaminated. Because of the nature of the material, it is recommended that professionals be called in to do the relamination and to apply a matching color coat.

If at some time the entire interior needs to be resurfaced, the pool is drained, the surface is lightly sanded, and a whole new coat of plastic resin is applied. Cost for resurfacing a fiberglass shell is approximately $150.

SEASONAL CARE

During the off-season — months when there is little or no swimming — your pool will require less maintenance than during months of peak use. However, no matter how mild the climate, don't put off all pool cleaning with the intention of giving the pool a thorough cleaning in the spring. In most cases, you'll find that the resulting spring cleaning is more than you bargained for.

Draining your pool usually is a poor practice, whether you live in a cold climate or a warm one. An empty pool is heavy, but it can still float. Freezing can expand soil, and your pool will probably be better off with a frozen surface to counteract the pressure from surrounding frozen earth. Also, water protects the concrete shell from rapid expansion and contraction caused by winter-time temperature fluctuation.

Some owners lower the pool water level by 2 or 3 feet in winter, leaving enough water so the pool will not float. But this usually is poor practice, because wet or frozen soil exerts the most pressure against the top of a pool. In addition, a plastered pool will almost inevitably end up with a stained ring around its sides at the lower water level.

Mild climates

In mild climates, you maintain your pool in the off-season just as you do in the summer — but not quite so often. With swimming at a minimum, the demand for filtration, chemical treatment, and a general cleanup is greatly reduced. You may have a few difficult weeks when leaves are falling during late autumn, but consistently cold temperatures and minimum activity generally relieve you of most maintenance chores.

Turn off your heater but, depending on the type of heater, leave the pilot light burning to prevent collection of moisture in the lines. Check with your equipment supplier first, as this procedure may not be recommended for your particular heater. The filter cycle can safely be cut to about half of the summer routine. Check pH and chlorine residual weekly, and add chemicals when needed. Keep the skimmer clean and the filter properly serviced. Brush the pool walls whenever they look dirty and vacuum occasionally to keep the pool floor in good condition.

Many pool owners cut even these chores down to a minimum by installing a tight-fitting cover (see page 27) that keeps leaves and dirt from getting into the water and the need for chlorination at an absolute minimum.

POOL COVER keeps leaves and dirt from getting into water, cutting down on off-season maintenance chores. This one also inflates to enclose pool for sheltered swimming (see photo on page 53).

If you have a diving board, cover it with a piece of canvas or plastic for protection.

Cold climates

In cold climates, pool builders in many cases take extra precautions during installation to make sure the pool can be winterized adequately. Your builder should provide you with a set of instructions for closing the pool.

The filter and heater often are located at a lower level than the pool, so the entire system can be drained easily by closing valves or plugging the pipe openings in the pool walls and letting gravity do the work. An alternative is to locate the filter-heater on a bank or mound several feet above the pool level. Then the system can be drained back into the pool, and the water remaining in the piping can be blown from the lines with an air compressor.

When the filter and heater are placed level with the pool, the system's pipes can still be buried 2 or more feet below ground, except where they rise ver-

tically for above-ground hookups. Somewhere along these deep lines there should be stop-and-waste valves with curb boxes (pipe wells giving access to them). The valves can be operated with a long sprinkler valve handle. Closing them stops water from entering the system from the pool and opens their waste outlets to drain away the water.

With any method, drain the filter, pump and heater (these usually have drain plugs), and any other low spots or traps in the system. If no provision was made in the original installation for draining your filter-heater system, contact your equipment manufacturer or a service company for advice on how to winterize your particular system.

In extremely cold climates, some owners float clean logs or styrene foam planks in the water (away from tile and coping) to weaken the ice. A fiberglass pool does not need the logging.

On-ground vinyl-lined pools should be drained or covered for winter protection. A large inflated ball in the pool will absorb possible ice pressure.

GUNITE operator must direct pressurized mixture of cement and sand in an even thickness over steel reinforcing rods. Surveying instruments are used to check wall alignment. Gunite is one of four main types of concrete pool construction.

POOL CONSTRUCTION

Pool construction falls into two general phases — the formation of a basic structure to hold water and the application of the finish and trim.

The structural element is, of course, the most important. Few if any shortcuts can be taken in engineering, design, and workmanship, or construction materials. An ill-advised savings in materials or the use of unskilled labor often results in later maintenance problems or actual pool failure.

The second phase of construction allows more freedom. You can select plaster, paint, tile, coping, and decking for economy, color, and personal taste. But haphazard methods are still to be avoided. While remodeling of this phase is possible, it is likely that whatever trim is applied to the pool — and how it is applied — will be with you for the life of the pool.

This section on construction procedures is not intended as a comprehensive do-it-yourself manual. It is rather a guide to help you understand the techniques and problems of pool construction. If you wish to embark on an owner-builder plan, this section can help you decide which phases of the work you are suited to do and which jobs are for professionals. You can't build a pool merely by following the descriptions on these pages. Each pool requires its own engineering and structural drawings, which must be designed for your location and site conditions. But by knowing ahead of time what problems you are likely to encounter, you will be better prepared for the job.

WHICH POOL FOR YOU?

There is no easy answer to the question of which type of swimming-pool construction is best suited to your particular needs. Price, personal taste, and availability of materials all must be considered.

Despite the many types of pools now being constructed, you may find that local competition and cost of materials limit the selection available to you.

The popularity of one type of pool may push it to the forefront as the most economical; or one construction method may have been forced completely off the market in your area because it was used by disreputable contractors or was not competitively priced. Check in the yellow pages of the phone book to find pool companies and contractors and what types of pools they build.

All pools discussed here — regardless of materials used in construction — can be engineered as sound structures. Some types are longer-lasting, others offer economy of construction, but all can be designed as adequate containers for water. No single type can be considered "best" for all situations.

The cost range

Pool costs depend on local conditions. It is relatively simple to estimate expenditures for equipment and accessories, but construction does not fit a standard pattern. The price of materials, labor situations, and competition within the industry are the major factors affecting total cost.

In general, vinyl liners are the least expensive pools and steel the most expensive. Between these are the various forms of concrete and fiberglass. Block pools are considered the most economical of the concrete methods, but usually this is because they are constructed by owner-builders. Gunite generally costs less than poured concrete, but it depends on which type of construction is most available. Fiberglass is usually on a par with gunite in cost but again locality is a factor.

This range is based on normal conditions, a level site, no soil problems, and standard pool shapes and sizes. It involves initial outlay only and not the life of the pool or maintenance costs.

Most contractors and pool companies offer "package" pools. By combining pool, filter system, tile, coping, interior finish, and accessories into one sale, they can offer a lower price than if you bought these elements separately. But if you vary from the basic package, the price fluctuates. In an owner-builder plan you may find the cost of materials, labor, and equipment more than it is for a contractor who has a sizable volume.

A check with pool builders will reveal the price range for pools in your area. When obtaining estimates, be sure you know what is included and what will cost extra. Pool prices are lowest in certain metropolitan areas, where competition is keenest. Costs generally are higher to both builder and buyer in regions where pool building is less popular or where freezing conditions make heavier structures necessary. The distance the builder must travel to the site also affects price.

In some areas you can obtain a better price during the winter when pool building is slack. But if you live in an area of severe winter climates, builders may refuse to build a pool at all or will charge more because of the extra problems involved. Some contractors in cold areas use tents to extend the construction season.

SELECTING THE BUILDER

Once you've decided that you definitely want a swimming pool you can turn the whole job over to professionals, do some of the work yourself and contract for jobs too technical or backbreaking, or do it all yourself. The latter method requires some careful thinking, thorough investigation, and a lot of energy.

Shopping for your pool

Buying a pool from a reputable pool company or contractor is the easiest, most trouble-free, and safest way. Building a pool is not like pouring a sidewalk or patio or working with non-bearing surfaces. Pools set below grade hold many tons of water and involve expenditures that warrant the best possible job. Correcting a pool failure is expensive, if not impossible. Choosing a reputable builder assures you of proper construction, and if any problems arise the builder will stand behind his work.

By all means shop around. Obtain competitive prices, making sure each estimate is based on exactly the same equipment, types and sizes of pipe, square footage of pool area, accessories and trim, and requirements for utilities and clean-up. Have everything in writing; implied specifications or verbal agreements can lead to misunderstandings.

Select the most qualified and reliable firm available in your area. The National Swimming Pool Institute, in conjunction with the majority of pool companies, is establishing standards for the trade, but there are still some unreliable firms who indulge in questionable practices. The worst that can happen is for a contractor to fail to complete the job according to the lien laws of some states. Unpaid subcontractors can file liens against the property, and the pool owner is then obliged to pay the money due for goods and services, even though he may already have paid once through the general contractor.

The contract

Before signing a contract, check carefully on the integrity of the contractor or pool company. The size and name of the company should not deter you from making a thorough check. Ask for a bank reference, and then check the contractor's method of payment to subcontractors and suppliers. Contact the local agency of your state's Contractors' Licensing Board to see if he has a proper license and is properly bonded with the state. Check the Better Business Bureau for information on his business practices. If you stipulate a performance completion and payment bond, be sure both aspects are covered, since a performance bond alone will not free you from liens by subcontractors. However, the bond will raise the cost; if there is an established pool builder with an outstanding reputation, it may not be necessary.

Your final contract should include a progressive payment program, with the total cost broken into three or four stages to be paid as they are completed. The contract should include a firm completion date and a detailed description of the pool structure, dimensions, and location on your lot. Check specifications to make sure they include correct piping lengths and square footage of walks and patios needed to complete the plan.

Brand names of filter, plumbing, heater, and other equipment and accessories should be stated clearly. (The use of equipment approved by the National Sanitation Foundation is recommended.) Make sure there is also a firm estimate on utility hookups, clear-cut cancellation provisions, satisfactory equipment guarantees, and an explanation of who fills the pool and starts the equipment working satisfactorily.

The owner-builder plan

Building part or all of your swimming pool can be a wise or a disastrous decision, depending on your own skills and the construction circumstances. Very few pools are built entirely by home owners. But a number of owners do part of the work themselves and contract the jobs for which they are not qualified.

Some equipment companies cater to owner-builders. If you buy all your equipment from one of these companies, they will provide plans, engineering specifications, plenty of free advice, and supervision of the job. If you have problems, they will attempt to solve them, though the costs remain with you. All owner-builders should locate a source of professional advice, through engineering firms, designers, equipment manufacturers, or representatives of accredited pool companies.

Before attempting an owner-builder plan, collect all the information available on the type of pool you plan to build. Study plans, brochures, and catalogs for design ideas, construction pointers, and cost estimates.

You'll need a set of construction specifications signed by an engineer registered in your state, and these plans must be approved by the local building department. Obtain all necessary building permits and find out at what stages of construction an inspector is required.

The amount of work an owner-builder can actually do himself partially depends on the type of pool. Only two types are suitable for the amateur — concrete masonry block and vinyl-lined.

With concrete block you can work at a slow pace, and the construction details are not too complex. No special equipment is needed, and the company that sells you the blocks will also provide plans (if plans are not available locally, you can obtain a set by writing to the National Concrete Masonry Association — 2009 North 14th Street, Arlington, Virginia 22201 — or to some vinyl liner manufacturers). The strength of a block pool is not dependent on a monolithic pour, and its design enables the amateur to work only on weekends without endangering the structure.

Vinyl-lined pools are the most practical for the owner-builder. You can either tackle the whole job yourself, contract the rough work and install the liner yourself, or hire a contractor to do the whole job. There are kits for the entire pool, including wood, steel, or aluminum side walls; these are designed particularly for owner-builders and are quite practical where shipping costs are not prohibitive.

EXCAVATING THE SITE

The first step in pool construction — and in many cases the most important — is the excavation into which the swimming pool is poured, gunned, or dropped. How the excavation is formed can have an effect on the resulting shape and strength of the pool.

A contract signed with a pool company or contractor will usually include the cost of the excavation and removal and disposal of the dirt. If your property cannot accommodate a 6 to 8-foot minimum access for heavy equipment, the costs for excavation will run higher. Access areas less than 5 feet wide will necessitate hand digging, at costs that could be prohibitive.

During the planning stage of your pool, consider the possibility of using some of the excess dirt for landscaping purposes, such as a mound for planting

CONSTRUCTION begins with excavation; a 6 to 8-foot access width is needed for heavy equipment used.

or a raised patio area. It won't make any difference in your costs.

If you want to dig the excavation yourself, talk to someone who has already done it. Excavating for a pool is a dirty, backbreaking job. Here are some general tips:

- Know where buried utility lines are.
- Be sure you aren't in danger of running into rock or water.
- Have plenty of willing hands, or the job will take weeks.
- Have a convenient place to dispose of the dirt, or the cost of hauling will erase any saving.
- Have a supervisor for the finishing: a paid representative of the company building the pool, your building materials supplier, or a representative of a pool equipment supplier.

Soil conditions

Pool shells vary as to type of construction, but each is basically a container built to hold many tons of water. Consequently, your pool builder must consider the soil conditions surrounding the structure. Pool walls must counteract soil pressures so the pool will not crack inward, even when empty. At the same time they must hold the water in the pool regardless of the fluctuations in ground pressure due to moisture changes and weak spots, so the pool will not buckle or crack outward.

In-ground pools must be designed to resist earth pressures when the pool is empty; although draining

PLASTIC HEADERS may be imbedded between deck sections to permit flexibility in expansive soil.

a pool is not recommended if it can be avoided, all pools at one time or another are empty for curing, painting, refinishing, or cleaning. There also may be other circumstances that require special design or preventive measures, and failure to recognize them could lead to early pool failure.

Local pool companies and contractors usually are familiar with the soil conditions in your area. Some contractors specialize in difficult jobs, while others will simply state that they are not qualified to handle the problem.

Problem soils. There are three types of soil problems — water, rock, and sand. If they are encountered in the excavation, you can expect the cost to double or triple.

Water is a problem because the loader can't move about freely, the walls sag, and the finishing cannot be done. One solution is to pump the water out while the pool excavation is in progress until the main drain is set. Water can then be pumped out through the main drain until the shell is in and proper drainage is provided. If water prevents the loader from entering the pool at all, it may be necessary for the contractor to use a clam shovel — a machine that sits outside the pool and scoops the mud out of the bottom. Too much water may be a good reason for not building the pool at all if adequate drainage cannot be arranged.

Dynamite or air hammers can be used on rock, depending on the size of the problem. This can be extremely expensive, since the contractor must keep a loader on the job to move the rock as it is chipped away. Aside from the expense, rock is a distinct advantage because it provides a solid foundation for the pool.

If the excavation turns up sand, walls may cave in as the excavation deepens. There usually is a stopping point for cave-ins, but if the trouble persists, a thin coat of gunite sometimes is sprayed on the walls to shore them up until the pool shell is built.

An empty pool can float

Pools with rigid floors sometimes are subject to underground water pressure. The pool is basically a giant saucer and can be pushed upward if enough water pressure is allowed to collect beneath it. This is particularly dangerous when the pool is empty, since there is only the weight of the structure to counteract the pressure.

A hydrostatic valve is installed at the main drain (and sometimes other areas) to relieve the water pressure if the pool must be drained. The valve remains closed while the pool is full, but when the pool is either partially or completely drained, it is opened to allow ground water to enter the pool through the main drain. When the pool is refilled, the valve is again closed to prevent gravel from getting into the opening. Some pools require a leaching field as well as hydrostatic valves.

If a hydrostatic valve is not used, never drain the pool without first contacting the contractor or an engineer. He will advise when the water table is low enough to avoid a dangerous pressure build-up.

In all cases where there is likely to be a very heavy build-up of underground water, a sub-grade drainage system should be installed. A line of drain tile (4-inch diameter) can be set around the perimeter of the pool. The tile should be set on a definite grade for good drainage. The floor of a concrete or fiberglass pool should also be set on a bed of crushed rock, if surrounding soils are normally slow-draining.

Expansive soils

Certain types of soils will expand more than others when water-saturated. Adobe soil is particularly difficult to deal with; it resists water, but when it finally does absorb moisture it expands considerably. As a result, heavy pressure builds up against rigid concrete pool walls and may crack them.

Pool builders generally have two or more sets of plans for reinforcing steel for concrete shells, one for normal soils and one for expansive soils. The latter calls for more reinforcing steel, thicker walls, or both. But there is still a danger of cracking if the soil expansion is uneven or greater than anticipated.

A critical point of water seepage is between coping, bond beam, and walkway sections. Expansion joints and sealants usually are installed in these areas. A joint rims the pool vertically between regular coping and the walkway, and a sealant, usually rubber or plastic, is poured as a liquid into a gap prepared for it. When the liquid dries, it forms a tight, flexible seal. With cantilevered decking, the sealant is applied between the bond beam and the concrete decking. Usually a 6 to 12-inch lip is also poured on the back edge of the surrounding walkway to provide extra support for the bond beam as well as added protection against seepage.

If decks are laid out in sections, these joints must also be sealed for several feet around the pool. Preformed plastic headers, shaped to allow flexibility, can be imbedded between the concrete sections.

Either the ground should slope away from the pool or a drainage system should be provided to prevent water from collecting in puddles around the pool. If the drainage problem is severe there are other preventive measures:

• A trench, 4 feet deep and 12 inches wide, can be dug around the pool 5 to 10 feet from the walls and filled with loose material that can absorb the soil expansion. The top of the trench can be covered with decking later so it will not show.

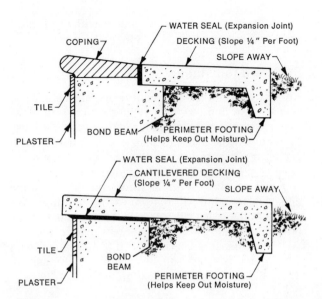

TYPICAL expansion joint treatment is shown for separate coping and decking, cantilevered decking.

• The top 3 feet of clay around a pool, under the walkway, can be replaced with clean, compacted fill. This lessens the pressure by removing the cause.

Under freezing conditions. If only occasional light freezing occurs in your locality, engineering specifications will not vary from those used in mild-weather climates. Otherwise, piping should be buried below the frost line, or drains provided, and special precautions must be taken to protect equipment and the pool's interior finish.

In areas where there is considerable freezing, pool design must allow for the extra pressures that result in winter soil expansion. Thicker walls, heavier steel reinforcing, and the use of calcium additives in concrete to increase the density may be prescribed by the pool engineer.

Backfilling

When the area or depth of an excavation is great, engineered backfill is required. If the pool does not have a footing in solid earth, it will "float" in the fill. When the fill is compressed by the pool's weight and settles, the pool settles with it. If this settlement is uniform, the pool is apt to crack away from the bond beam and decking. If there is uneven settling, the pool will crack crosswise at approximately the 5-foot depth mark.

There are two general methods of giving the pool a solid footing:

• Make the pool deeper than originally planned, continuing the excavation until solid ground is reached.

• Use underpinning construction, whereby pilings or piers are sunk through the fill into solid ground.

The pool shell is tied to these pilings with reinforcing steel and a monolithic concrete pour.

Rock as a foundation

Normal granitelike rock requires expensive excavation but is a fine bed for a swimming pool. In areas where there is slate, shale, sand, and gravel — usually on slopes and hillsides — you must have a geologist's report before the engineering is done. These types of rocks tend to move and slide when wet and can impose great forces on the pool; the engineer probably will require extra retaining walls and perhaps a backfill of solid earth. The specific type of soil the geologist finds will dictate the preventative measures necessary. If a pool is on solid rock or undisturbed soil, a cushion of compacted, drainable material should be provided.

THE SHELL THAT HOLDS THE WATER

Swimming pools can be completely or partially below grade, anchored to hillsides, or placed directly on the surface of the ground. The type you select will determine construction methods and materials for your pool.

The majority of pools are fully in-ground structures. The convenience of access to water, and from the water to patio areas, makes the surface-level pool most popular. It also is the most adaptable to unified landscaping plans. This does not mean that the other types of construction cannot be attractive and enjoyable additions to your property. Location, soil conditions, and cost usually are the determining factors for choosing hillside and above-ground pools.

The most common types of pools available are concrete (gunite and poured), vinyl, fiberglass, and metal, or combinations of some of these.

Concrete pools

Concrete is the most popular construction material for swimming pools. Its workability, strength, and permanence make it ideal for below-grade pools.

The material is reinforced with steel rods to help resist the pressures of soil and water. The type and size of the steel will vary with location and structural requirements.

The four main types of concrete construction are gunite, poured, hand-packed, and block. Which of these is used depends on costs and available equipment and materials.

Gunite. Gunite is a mixture of hydrated cement and sand, applied over and under the steel reinforcing rods, directly against the soil. The mix is very dry and is "shot" from a nozzle under pressure to form a one-piece shell that is considered stronger than any other type of concrete.

With gunite there is complete freedom of size and shape, since the gunite follows any excavated shape. Gunite is one of the most practical methods for pool companies and contractors to mass-produce swimming pools. Also, the excavation is neat and does not require backfilling with subsequent danger of settling around the pool. The initial cost of gunite equipment and problems of transporting the rig make it impractical for the small contractor who builds only a few pools a year, so if you live away from a metropolitan area, you may find either that gunite is not available or that the cost may be higher than in a large city.

A gunite rig includes a large compressor, a transit mixer for combining the cement and sand, and a hose and mixing nozzle. The mix is forced through the nozzle, where it is combined with water, and actually blown against the excavation over a grid of reinforcing steel shaped around the interior of the excavation.

The shell must be of the proper thickness or weak spots can develop that will be unable to resist earth and hydrostatic pressures. Most operators place steel rods in the wall to measure the thickness. Some building inspectors may recommend that corings be taken to judge both mix and wall thickness.

The gunite must be directed behind the steel against the earth, so the nozzle man must be careful that pockets of air or loose sand do not form. Loose sand that rebounds from the nozzle must be picked up by an assistant or it can form weak spots in the structure.

Occasionally the operator, busy regulating the mix and applying the gunite, may seal up a pipe inlet. The main drain, inlet lines, and vacuum lines should be checked immediately after the gunite crew is finished to be sure the lines are open. Plastic covers or plugs sometimes are placed over the openings before guniting. Afterwards the covers are simply removed, leaving the lines open and clean.

Gunite has a rough texture and must be hand-trimmed before plaster or paint is applied. Finishers move in immediately after the gunite crew to trim the walls and floors. They also cut skimmer openings if a precast unit is not used, clean out the light niche, and dry-pack any small crevices that appear. Steps are gunited at the same time as the pool structure.

Poured concrete. Before the use of gunite, poured concrete was the most popular method of constructing pools, but many companies have abandoned this method because of the labor involved in setting the forms and the time it takes for the concrete to set. Some have adopted forms fabricated into popular shapes and reusable for several pools each season; sizes and shapes are governed by the forms available. "Flexible" forms that can be used to create

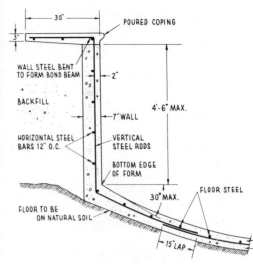

FOR POURED CONCRETE pool, bottom end of forms is dammed up until the concrete stiffens. Floor is poured directly and tamped down around reinforcing bars. Vertical bars are bent flat and tied to those in decking.

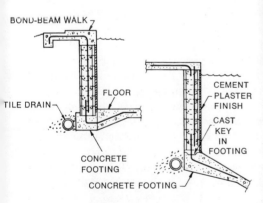

MASONRY BLOCK construction is similar to that for poured concrete, with the blocks serving as forms. Drawings show two ways of starting wall. At left, bottom row of blocks is set in footing; at right, a key is cast in footing to match bottom row of blocks.

free-form shapes have been developed, but in most cases you are limited to a rectangular, teardrop, or kidney shape.

When piping has been stubbed in, the outside forms for the walls generally are put into position. Steel reinforcing is then placed according to the engineer's specifications — similar to those for a gunite shell. Bars should overlap according to specifications and should not bear against the outside forms. For maximum strength, small concrete spreaders often are used to hold the steel in place.

Usually the inside forms are then locked in place. Special couplings used between the forms for vacuum and inlet lines are firmly embedded in the concrete walls; the couplings may be filled with grease to keep out the concrete until the pool is finished and face plates can be attached. A wooden frame can be inserted between the forms for the skimmer.

Most contractors use a dry mix of cement, sand, and rock which gives the vertical walls uniform strength and a smooth finish. It is also necessary on the floor when the concrete must be placed by hand on a slope. The floor is poured with a build-up on the corners, then troweled and floated.

When the forms have been removed, piping is completed, the walls cleaned and scrubbed, and the pool backfilled with clean, solidly-packed fill around the outside. Pouring of the bond beam (top portion of wall, widened and steel-reinforced for added strength) may be the last structural step, unless it is incorporated with the basic pour. Steel rods projecting from the pool walls are bent down and tied to reinforcing rods in the bond beam.

Hand-packed concrete. In most parts of the United States, hand-packing a concrete pool has become practically obsolete. Basically, hand-packed concrete is the same as poured concrete, only most of the forms are eliminated. The concrete can be dumped directly into the pool from the transit mixer. After each load is dumped, it must be worked into shape immediately. The concrete mix is tossed against the excavation and stacked by hand to form the walls.

Since there is no way of regulating the concrete flow, the strength of the pool depends on the ability of the workers; rehandling and overworking the concrete must be avoided. Careful attention to detail is required.

A disadvantage of hand-packed pools is that they have sloping sides, which are inconvenient for swimmers getting out of the pool and do not lend themselves to competitive swimming.

Masonry blocks. Concrete block pools are similar to poured pools, with the blocks serving as forms. The blocks can either be mortar-set or interlocking; the interlocking ones are easier to handle, and no spe-

cial talents are required to stack them into walls. Few pool companies build block pools, but small contractors sometimes find this is the most economical construction method without a heavy capital outlay for equipment.

Because of the rectangular shape of the blocks, most pools of this type have straight lines — rectangular, wedge-shaped, or L-shaped. Curves can be incorporated into the design but should not have less than a 10-foot radius.

After the excavation is completed and the main drain and line are set, a continuous reinforced concrete footing is poured around the perimeter to serve as a base for the walls (this may be incorporated with the floor). The footings must be level, solid, and in strict accordance with the engineer's specifications. Usually 12 by 12-inch or 8 by 24-inch, they are reinforced with steel rods extending into the floor and up into the walls.

Two methods of starting the walls are shown on page 91. The wall at left has the bottom row of blocks set in the footing; this is the best method for starting the first row if the entire course can be set while the footings are still workable. At right, a key is cast in the footing to match the bottom row of blocks; this method is used when the first row of blocks cannot be placed until after the footing has set.

Working from the deep-end corners permits stacking uphill to form the floor slope. The bottom block is set and each higher block overlapped to create a staircase effect. A rubber mallet can be used to pound each block into place; the blocks must be checked immediately for accurate positioning. An unnoticed error will be multiplied as the height of the wall increases. When the entire first course is laid, the blocks are filled with grout to provide a solid joint with the footing.

As the walls go up, openings must be left for plumbing, underwater light, and skimmer opening. Blocks should be set to within 8 inches of the top of the wall; above this the bond beam is poured.

The floor can be poured when the walls are completed or at the same time the footing is poured. Steel is tied to the rods projecting from the wall footings to form a solid mesh. The floor should be poured monolithically and troweled to a smooth finish. The bond beam is the last construction element to be formed; on block pools the beam may be up to 3 feet wide, 6 to 8 inches thick, and tied to the block walls by bending down the steel rods projecting from the walls.

An interior finish must be applied to a masonry block pool to provide a waterproof surface for plaster and paint finishes. (See page 98; also see the section on vinyl-lined pools, page 95.)

GALVANIZED STEEL panel is moved into position to be bolted to corner section for steel pool. At right, installer attaches an 'A' frame at joint of two panels for added strength.

Metal pools

The advantage of metal pools is their strength. In residential pools they are used primarily for problem sites such as hillsides or loose fill and areas of heavy freezing. Installation time is much shorter than for concrete, but the cost is higher.

Both steel and aluminum have become popular in the above-ground pool market. Most interiors are vinyl-lined. In the case of steel, the outside walls are usually finished with baked-on enamels in wood-grain or pastel colors to match the landscape.

Steel. All steel pools, whether exposed or buried, are constructed to hold the water without help from soil. Steel pools are ¼-inch plate, constructed in straight or curved panels at the manufacturer's plant. In many cases the piping, fitting, steps, light niche, and skimmer outlet are built in the basic frame. When the pool is delivered to the site, it is ready to be bolted and welded.

Because of the size of the steel sections, access can be a problem. Trucks to haul the steel and a crane to position it must be moved fairly close to the pool. The pool exterior is strongly braced, bolted, and welded — projecting anchors tie the frame to the decking. Steel side walls are available in galvanized, porcelainized, or stainless steel; each material is available in several shapes and sizes.

Aluminum. Aluminum pools, like steel pools, are excellent below-grade structures because of their strength. Prefabricated panels and structural components are shipped to the site ready for installation. Residential pools, both above and below-grade, may have vinyl-lined interiors (see following section on vinyl-lined pools).

VINYL LINER is placed in position for several helpers to install it. Because of the exacting fit required, rectangles and ovals are the most popular shapes for vinyl-lined pools.

WRINKLES ARE REMOVED by using a special vacuum cleaner that pulls air from behind the liner (left) before the pool is filled with water, then smoothing with soft-bristled broom as water rises in the pool.

Vinyl-lined pools

Vinyl liners are waterproof plastic interior skins for swimming pools. Though the liner is sometimes referred to as a type of pool, it actually is a covering which must be supported by walls and rest on a solid sand base. Its chief attraction lies in its low cost, both for installation and maintenance. Vinyl is resistant to the black algae that create problems on concrete, plaster, or painted surfaces.

The watertight liners are fabricated from 20-mil sheets of vinyl plastic. The only problem involved in fabrication is in the sealing of the seams; to insure a perfect bond, seams must be fused tightly to resist stretching and water pressure. Reliable fabricators have solved this problem, and separation of seams seldom occurs. A range of colors is available, but the most popular still is an aqua or a light blue.

How long a liner will last has not been definitely established. Reputable manufacturers will guarantee a liner against defective workmanship for 10 years. Its wearing powers are largely determined by environment and proper care. Direct sunlight on the section of the liner above water and pool alkalinity have a bearing on its durability. Chemicals do not affect it, unless by some chance chlorinated tablets are allowed to rest directly on the material; chlorine is a bleach and can cause discoloration.

Numerous vinyl liner pool builders, dealers, and distributors offer complete pool installation or sell kits to owner-builders. Sizes range from 8 by 16 feet to 25 by 50 feet, with a deep hopper for diving. Free-form, bowed-end, and L-shape pools are available, but rectangles and ovals are the most popular because of a shaped liner's exacting requirements for manufacture and installation.

Coping varies with each type of construction, and each manufacturer has his own method of anchoring the liner. All types of aluminum, cement, and steel pools are manufactured for easy liner replacement if necessary.

There are two construction phases — the building of the shell and the installation of the liner. The basic framework can be of any durable material — concrete, wood, steel, or aluminum. The frame need not be waterproof, since the liner is, but it must be structurally adequate and have a smooth surface so the liner will not be abraded.

For those who wish to build their own pool, a vinyl liner may be the best choice. Complete kits with detailed instructions for wood, galvanized steel, or aluminum wall construction allow the home owner to control all aspects of the construction, contracting for the more specialized tasks such as the excavation.

Poured concrete walls. Because of the expense and labor involved in forming the walls, poured concrete is no longer used to any extent. Contractors normally work with re-usable forms, so the sizes and shapes are limited.

Concrete block. Block walls for liner pools are basically the same as those for regular concrete block pools (see page 92). Though the structure does not have to be leakproof, the walls must be covered with a plaster material so there are no rough spots or corners that could cause wear to the liner. An acoustical plaster material sometimes is used by masonry block contractors for both walls and bottom, providing a smooth surface as well as insulation.

The liner must fit the exact measurements of the pool, so manufacturers have developed standardized sizes to fit plans for block-wall pools.

Wood. Panels of specially treated wood are used in many vinyl liner pools. Wood should never be creosote-treated or it will destroy the vinyl. Available kits contain all the material needed, including the liner, and explicit installation instructions.

Steel. Panels of 1/8-inch welded galvanized steel, bolted together, are used to form the side walls. The panels are imbedded in concrete footings and reinforced with "A" frames at the joints to withstand water pressure without the help of compacted backfill. The vinyl liner snaps into the coping. A vacuum cleaner may be used to suck out the air between liner and walls, eliminating wrinkles.

Aluminum. Aluminum shells with vinyl liners are available in a number of sizes and shapes, including free-form. Coping is of concrete or aluminum, specifically manufactured to receive the vinyl liner. The pool can be fully contracted, or kits with complete instructions are available for owner-builders.

Tips for owner-builders. Steel, wood, and aluminum frames are used in above-ground liner pools. These kits are easily assembled, with interlocking panels forming the basic frame. The pools also are easy to disassemble and may be taken down in the winter and stored.

Installation of an in-ground vinyl-lined pool is not simple. The pools come with detailed instructions, but it will be helpful if you can watch a few other pools being installed. Excavation is especially important; there must be a stable ledge of earth for the walls to rest on. You will probably save money in the long run by having a dealer offering a kit plan arrange for the excavation, delivery of the equipment, and an owner-paid supervisor. Creating a masonry block shell or setting wood or metal framework is difficult and exacting, since the liner must fit perfectly. Placing the liner is a job for three or four men.

Excavation for in-ground metal or wood walls can be over-cut 12 to 24 inches on the sides, down to the shelf of undisturbed earth required for setting the

FIBERGLASS-WALLED pool has concrete bottom. Wall panels still have protective paper covering in photo.

ONE-PIECE fiberglass pool is lifted into place by crane; built-in steps are visible on the right side.

walls. When the excavation is complete, the side walls are placed. Walls correctly engineered, constructed, and installed must be vertical and true to the measurements of the liner; otherwise you will have trouble positioning the liner. Backfilling the walls varies according to the type of installation.

The bottom of the pool is usually a 2 to 3-inch bed of sand. Have the surface smooth and level, with no pits or lumps. On the slope toward the deep end the sand can be saturated and tamped into position.

If you are setting the liner yourself, be sure you understand the manufacturer's directions before you start. Unfold the liner in a warm place to let the packaging wrinkles work themselves out, then have as many people as possible help you drop it into the hole. The use of a special vacuum to suck the air out between the liner and wall is recommended by some manufacturers to help eliminate wrinkles and to seat the liner properly. The liner should stretch into place as the pool fills with water, and all wrinkles must be removed as you go. Above all, avoid a situation where the pool must be drained and the liner re-fitted. It is next to impossible to reseat the stretched vinyl satisfactorily.

Except for the main drain, openings in the liner should not be cut to accommodate fittings until the water is just below the place where the hole will be made. If the holes for skimmer, lights, and inlet lines

are made too soon, the liner may stretch and tear. Be very careful when cutting the liner; you may accidentally cut a leak in the vinyl.

Vinyl liner pools with wood or metal walls do not need to be excavated for full in-ground installation. Some pools are built with the surface decking a foot or more above ground; less excavation is needed, and the above-ground portion can be decked and landscaped in a terraced effect.

Fiberglass pools

Major improvements in construction and installation techniques for fiberglass pools have overcome the original problems of leaking, buckling, and adverse reaction of the material to soil chemicals. The biggest advantage of a fiberglass pool is low maintenance; black algae cannot cling to the surface, and chemical needs are held to a minimum. Color can be built right into the material, so no other interior finish is required.

Fiberglass has a high tensile strength and flexibility, making it particularly adaptable in areas where there is severe freezing or in expansive soil conditions. The nature of the material precludes the need for an expansion joint around the pool, though deck sections should have expansion headers if the soil is expansive, the same as for concrete pools.

INSTALLED one-piece fiberglass pool has coping incorporated into pool shell, eliminating the need for separate coping. Ease of maintenance has made fiberglass popular as a pool material.

Two types of fiberglass pools are available: one-piece shells complete with steps and coping, and fiberglass-walled pools with poured concrete floor, vinyl coping, and water-line tile.

The one-piece shells are presently available in only a few parts of the country, but licensed manufacturing plants being established in various localities will extend the market for these pools. In general, construction involves an upside-down mold over which a releasing agent is applied so that the finished pool will not stick to its mold. A gelcoat containing the finish color is applied, and alternating layers of fiberglass matt and roving are laminated over the mold to the desired thickness. Each layer of glass cloth is saturated with resin and combines with the gelcoat, creating a homogenous unit.

After excavation is completed the shell is delivered to the site by truck and trailer, then hoisted by crane (right over the house, if necessary) and lowered into the excavation. Special fittings made specifically for fiberglass pools are installed with proper sealants. The concrete decking and bond beam (when used) is a one-piece pour which incorporates the coping (see photograph above).

The major disadvantage of the one-piece fiberglass pool is the present limitation in size and shape. The largest manufacturer offers only two models —

one 34 feet long and 16 feet wide in the middle, tapering to 14 feet at both ends, and another 26 by 12 feet tapering to 11 feet. Depths range from 3 to 9 feet. Transporting the shells by truck and trailer is subject to state and local highway restrictions.

Fiberglass-walled pools are constructed of prefabricated panels bolted and sealed together at the pool site to form a continuous 3-foot wall. The panels are multi-laminated fiberglass with a gelcoat finish and steel-rib reinforcement. Since the panels can be flexible, virtually any size or shape of pool can be built.

The wall base is embedded in a poured concrete footing. After the panels are in place, the pool floor and steps are formed of steel-reinforced poured concrete, and standard fittings are installed with the proper sealants. A special vinyl coping is inserted, and when the decking is poured the concrete is worked into the curved lip of the coping. Mosaic tile is applied as trim. The floor usually is finished with a masonry-type waterproof coating, or it can be painted.

The wall-panel method of construction allows more mobility and variety in size and shape than one-piece shells, but the advantages of fiberglass — easier maintenance and greater flexibility — are limited to the walls of the pool and elimination of perimeter expansion joints in expansive soils.

FINISHING THE POOL

Vinyl liner and one-piece fiberglass pools and the panels in fiberglass-walled pools need no interior finish. All others must be plastered or painted (tile finishes are seldom seen on residential pools because of the high cost of materials and labor). Plastering is a job for a professional; paint can be applied by the home owner. However, paint must be handled carefully when applied to a surface that is to be submerged. It is usually best to consult a reliable paint manufacturer before deciding whether to do it yourself.

Tile for trim usually is used around the perimeter of a pool beneath the coping and many times is set into the floor and/or risers of steps for additional color. Coping serves several purposes: It gives the pool a good finish, covering the bond beam and any steel projecting from pool walls; it emphasizes the lines of the pool; and it forms a hand-hold for swimmers. Coping will help drainage — correctly installed stone is positioned so water splashed out of the pool will flow away into drainage channels in the deck.

Paint

In most parts of the United States, it is less expensive to paint than to plaster a pool. However, a painted pool does require additional coats every few years, whereas a properly maintained plaster finish may last indefinitely in mild climates.

Four basic types of paint are presently used for swimming pools: cement base, chlorinated rubber base, vinyl, and epoxy. Cement base paint is the least expensive (about $40 for two coats on a 16 by 34-foot pool) but will last only one year. The pool must be drained and repainted every spring to maintain a smooth finish. Cement paint is the easiest for the amateur to apply and usually is used under conditions where the pool will be drained every year anyway.

Chlorinated rubber paint is normally the most practical and economical. It is generally considered more attractive than cement base paint and lasts somewhat longer. It is less expensive and much easier to apply than vinyl or epoxy paints.

Vinyl paint gives a hard, glossy surface that has greater abrasion resistance than chlorinated rubber paint. Vinyl also dries much faster, although it requires a brushed primer coat and spray application. If you use either chlorinated rubber or vinyl, you can expect to apply a fresh coat over the old paint every two or three years.

Epoxy paint produces a very good finish but is so difficult to handle that the home owner would be wise not to attempt applying it himself but to call in an expert.

Concrete. In some areas, few concrete pools are painted because of the quality and low price of plaster finishes that are available. In other regions, paint is recommended by contractors as the most practical finish. Talk to other pool owners and pool service men in your area to find which finish is more economical in the long run.

Preparation for painting varies depending on climate, type of paint, and personal experience. Contractors may or may not recommend acid washing, scrubbing, sandblasting, or curing. Best advice for painting concrete pools can be obtained directly from the manufacturer. Follow directions explicitly, and call a company representative if there are any problems.

Steel and aluminum. Chlorinated rubber paint is usually recommended for steel and aluminum pools.

With steel, five or six coats are required to cover the surface adequately and eliminate pin pointing or pinholes that could rust. A two-stage preparatory procedure must be followed. First, all ridges and welding marks must be ground off; if allowed to remain, they will push through the paint film and rust. Then the steel must be sandblasted the same day the primer coat is to be applied; this way all rust is removed and the primer can be applied before rusting can start again. Manufacturer's specifications should be consulted for type of primer to be used.

Steel must be repainted after the first year to cover pinholes that inevitably are missed with the first paint job. After one season, these pinholes show up as rust spots; they should be cleaned and touched up with paint, and then the entire pool should be given one more coat. This retouching generally is needed only after the first season. From then on, the pool should be repainted every two or three years.

Plaster

The most common finish for concrete pools is plaster, which lasts indefinitely (12 to 20 years minimum in a correctly maintained pool operated all year), gives a smooth waterproof "skin" to the pool, and provides a non-skid walking surface on the pool bottom.

Swimming-pool plaster is quite different from house plaster, requiring much more troweling and finishing than the household variety. Pool specialists are the only artisans qualified to do the job. The surface is first washed with muriatic acid and rinsed thoroughly; all water and acid are pumped from the pool before the plasterers can begin.

There are two major problems that must be overcome to ensure a good plaster job. First, pool plaster sets up rapidly and may crack if not worked properly and kept wet during the finishing operation. If a crack does appear after the plasterers are finished,

PLASTERING a pool is a job for a professional, since cracks or trowel burns can develop if the plaster is not worked properly. Plaster is the most common finish for concrete pools.

THE FINAL PART of the pool to be plastered is the steps. One plasterer is finishing the steps while the other removes his shoe "platforms" to leave the pool.

TILE SETTER first applies grout to top edge of pool wall, then presses tile into place on the grout.

CREVICES between the pieces of mosaic tile are filled in with grout applied over the tile.

EXCESS GROUT is washed off the surface of the tiles, leaving only the spaces between squares covered.

TILING around the surface skimmer requires special care; tile will be placed into opening and at bottom.

the surface loses its waterproof quality. Plaster cracks cannot always be repaired and still provide the clean appearance and waterproofing that is necessary. Reputable plasterers will refinish the entire pool if a crack appears.

Secondly, the continual troweling while the plaster is setting may cause trowel burns. If the white plaster turns only slightly brown, the burns can be washed out with acid. But if the burns show up as black smears, there is no way of removing them; you can either live with them or have the pool refinished.

Plastering a residential pool costs between $370 and $500, depending on the inside dimensions. On concrete block pools the joints must be covered with a coat of waterproof plastic cement and washed sand before the plaster is applied, adding another $100.

Tile trim

Tile trim for concrete pools usually is applied after the coping has been installed. The bottom of the coping stones serves as a guide for positioning the tile in a level line around the pool. There is a wide variety in size, shape, and color of tile for trim, both for the perimeter under the coping and mosaic designs set into the wall, steps, or pool bottom.

Tile-setting around the surface skimmer calls for extra care. The tile should reach into the skimmer opening to the weir that controls the flow of water. The bottom of the opening should also have a row of tile, with quarter-round used to cover the joints and sharp corners.

Coping

Standard coping stone, precast at a mixing plant and delivered to the pool site in 24-inch sections, is the most economical type of coping. Coping stones usually are made from colored concrete with a porous finish. Coping grout can be the same color as the stones or a complementing color.

Precast coping is priced from $1.50 to $3.25 per 24-inch stone, depending on color and finish. You can have it installed for approximately 70 to 80 cents per lineal foot. Corner stones and the curved stones needed for free-form pools are priced slightly higher.

The irregular shape of flagstone and the natural look given to a patio by its use can be carried to the water line of the pool. However, if this naturally-rough stone is used, the inside edges should be trimmed and buffed to eliminate all sharp corners. Some pool companies offer precast simulated rock coping which is less expensive than natural stone and is prebuffed for a smooth edging.

Cantilevered decks have become popular for many pool installations. The perimeter decking is shaped to eliminate the need for separate coping; the edges are smoothed to allow a safe hand-hold.

ROCKLIKE coping stones are cemented in place to give the pool the appearance of a natural pond.

POOL FILTER and heater are sheltered in an attractive structure where equipment can be reached easily. Heater stack projects above roof.

FILTER AND HEATER

The filter system is the only absolutely essential pool equipment. It enables you to use the initial water supply over and over again, adding only enough to make up for evaporation, backwashing, and splash-out. An efficient filter mixes sanitizing chemicals and cleans the water by filtering out unwanted debris. A good filter, plus normal chemical treatment and vacuuming, will guarantee that your pool remains sanitary and attractive.

The size of the filter is determined by the amount of water the pool holds (see page 74 for determining total pool capacity). It must be able to filter all the water in a reasonable time. Too small a filter will be over-taxed and fail to keep the pool clean. Too large a filter, on the other hand, will be needlessly expensive to install and operate. Residential pools of 800 square feet or less usually require only one filter tank to completely filter the total volume of water in the pool in 8 to 12 hours of continuous operation. The chart on page 107 shows types of filters and pumps required for most residential pools.

WHICH TYPE OF FILTER FOR YOU?

A filtration system is composed of four elements: the filter tank itself, a pump with hair and lint strainer, an automatic surface skimmer, and recirculating piping. The materials used in filters vary, but all parts should, if possible, be corrosion resistant — stainless steel, copper, bronze, plastic, or other non-ferrous material.

For residential pools there are two major types of

filters available: high rate sand and pressure diatomaceous earth. Rapid pressure sand and gravel filters, though still considered best by many engineers, are seldom used any more for pools in residential areas. The media (layers of sand and gravel) lasts for 10 to 15 years with normal care and requires very little maintenance; but the amount of water needed for backwashing and subsequent disposal is excessive. Sewer systems in many communities are already over-taxed, and in some cases pool connections are forbidden by law.

High rate sand filters

In recent years high rate sand filters have become popular for residential pools. These filters are pressure vessels, generally stainless steel or fiberglass in the small units (18 to 24-inch diameter) and steel in the larger ones. Special under drains and influent collection systems maintain a non-turbulent flow of pool water through the filtering media, which consists of special grades of sand. The flow rate operates up to 25 gallons per minute per square foot of filter bed area. Your filter supplier will recommend the proper grade for your particular unit.

The high rate filtering system is based on the concept that the high flow rates and pressures drive dirt particles down through the sand bed, giving maximum use of the filtering media. Theoretically, if the filter were not backwashed (cleaned), the dirt particles could reach the under drain, where they would then be directed back into the pool. Under normal conditions the pressure build-up is such that the

COMPLETE filtration system shown here includes diatomaceous earth filter (left rear), pump and motor (left foreground), separation tank for D.E. filter (center), direct-fired all-weather stackless heater (right), and automatic chlorinator (front).

pump flow is stopped before this happens. However, because of this possibility and the higher pressure pumps required in commercial installations, many local health agencies do not accept the high rate sand filter for public pools. Nevertheless, the units have been found to be quite satisfactory for filtering residential pools.

Backwashing the dirt out of the filter consists simply of turning the proper valves, allowing water to flow in reverse through the media. A high rate sand filter requires 50 to 60 gallons per minute (minimum) of water to backwash, with full pump output for 2 to 3 minutes. As with sand and gravel filters, the waste water must be disposed of, either through a sewer system or storm drain. If your local building codes require other sanitary means, the waste water can be diverted to a dry well where it will disperse slowly through seepage.

High rate sand filters lend themselves quite readily to automation. The filters of the future will likely be marketed with automatic backwash systems, eliminating a maintenance chore for the home owner.

High rate sand filters cost from $250 to $625, depending on size. This includes tank, pump and motor, valves and face piping, gauges, sight glass, and filter media. With proper care the sand media will not need to be replaced for several years. If there is clogging, replacement costs are minimal.

Diatomaceous earth filters

Diatomaceous earth filters have three advantages over sand filters: They are less expensive to install, they take up less space, and they are more modest in their backwashing demands.

This type of filter strains the water through diatomaceous earth, or D.E., a sedimentary rock composed of microscopic fossil skeletons of a small water animal, the diatom. The skeletons have a highly porous lattice structure of silica which makes them almost inert to any chemical action. The D.E. rock is mined and then crushed, washed, sized, and packed as a white, flourlike powder. The coarser sizes are more adaptable to swimming pool filtration; the particular grade best suited to your equipment will be recommended by the manufacturer.

The D.E. pressure filter has practically replaced the D.E. vacuum filter. These differ in most respects, except for the filtering element itself. The vacuum unit usually operates as both filter and surface skimmer. The filter pump sucks the water through the tank and the filter leaves, which are coated with diatomaceous earth. Pool water flows over a floating weir into the filter to replace the water being drawn out by the pump. A strainer assembly in front of the filter elements catches leaves and other floating debris that would clog the filter plates.

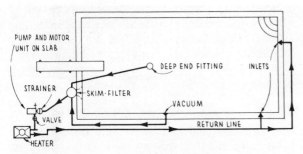

SKIM FILTER has all lines draining into skimmer; water is filtered, then drawn into pump for return to pool.

HIGH RATE sand filter at left is fiberglass; others may be made of stainless steel. At right is standard direct-fired heater. The shelter that houses the equipment is shown in photo on pages 102-103.

PRESSURE diatomaceous earth filter has horizontal tank, with filter elements arranged vertically. When properly applied, D.E. will completely cover the grids.

WATERFALL is return flow from filter-heater system of this pool. Landscape architect: John Michael.

Pressure D.E. units force the water through the filter media, much as the sand units do. Each septem (plate) has a filtering surface on both sides, and by increasing the number of plates, the filtering area is greatly increased without any appreciable enlargement of the tank. Costs range from $300 to $600.

A pressure filter does need backwashing, but only 75 gallons of water are usually required. Some pressure units are sold with separation tanks; the dirty water is backwashed through these tanks and filtered through fine-mesh bags. The cleansed water can then be returned to the pool and the dirty D.E. emptied out by hand. Such a tank often is necessary in areas where sewer connections are forbidden, since D.E. will clog a dry well and prevent dissipation of the water into the soil.

Pump and motor

The combination of pump and motor draws water from the pool, forces it through the filter, and sends it back to the pool.

The size of pump and motor is determined by the amount of water to be filtered, the rate at which it is to be filtered, and most important, the pressures at which the pump must perform. Enough horsepower should be provided to guarantee maximum filtration, but too much will damage the filter or the pump.

Horsepower alone is no gauge of the performance of a pump. The amount of water a pump will produce under specific back pressures — this is called the "pump head"— is the most important criterion of the pump's suitability.

Most filter systems come with pump and motor included as part of the package, and most pumps are self-priming centrifugal units. A regular centrifugal pump runs the danger of losing its prime, even if a small amount of air reaches the impellor. The pump must then be stopped immediately and reprimed by hand.

A hair and lint strainer is a standard feature of all self-priming units. It catches large particles of foreign matter before they enter and clog the pump impellor.

Installing the pump requires some care. It is recommended that pumps not be located more than 2 feet above pool water level or more than 35 to 40 feet away from the pool. If the filter location must be more than 40 feet away, the pump should be installed as close to the pool as possible.

Fractional horsepower motors, from ½ to 1½ horsepower, require single phase, 110/220 volt circuits. Although these motors can run on either voltage, it is best to use 220-volt current to prevent overloading the circuit when starting up. In many areas,

FILTERS, PUMPS, AND MOTORS

POOL SIZE IN FEET	APPROXI-MATE GALLON CAPACITY	SAND AND GRAVEL FILTERS				HIGH-RATE SAND FILTERS			PRESSURE D.E. FILTERS		
		Tank diameter	Filter area	Gallons per min.	Pump H.P.*	Filter area	Gallons per min.	Pump H.P.*	Filter area	Gallons per min.	Pump H.P.*
less than 15 x 30	less than 15,000	24"	3.14 sq. ft.	9-15	1/3	1.7 sq. ft.	25-30	1/2	15 sq. ft.	25-30	1/2
15 x 30 to 16 x 34	15,000 to 20,000	30"	4.9 sq. ft.	15-25	1/2	2-3 sq. ft.	35-50	3/4	20-25 sq. ft.	35-50	1/2-3/4
16 x 36 to 18 x 40	20,500 to 27,000	36"	7.07 sq. ft.	21-35	3/4	3-5 sq. ft.	45-60	1	30-35 sq. ft.	55-70	3/4-1
18 x 44 to 22 x 48	28,000 to 39,000	42"	9.6 sq. ft.	29-48	1	4.5 sq. ft.	70-80	1½	35-40 sq. ft.	65-80	1-1½

*Sand and gravel filters take low head pumps, high-rate sand and pressure D.E. take high head.

local ordinances require a special circuit for electrical motors. Even though most motors are dripproof, care should be taken that water does not rebound into the unit from the mounting platform surface, either by rain or hosing the area.

The surface skimmer

A surface skimmer is considered standard equipment by most swimming pool builders. Dirt, oils, lotions, and floating algae tend to collect on the surface of the water, and suction from the main drain outlet at the deepest point in the pool will not pull this material down. The skimmer, which draws only surface water, is installed to remove it.

The usual surface skimmer is made of aluminum, copper, brass, precast concrete, or plastic and consists of a round tank with a projecting throat on its upper side. A self-adjusting floating weir performs the skimming action. The weir regulates the amount of water that enters the skimmer. Because it adjusts itself to allow only a thin sheet of surface water to spill over it, velocity and not volume is the key to adequate skimming.

For fiberglass and vinyl pools, special skimmers with face plates and gaskets are available. Another type of skimmer, the "lily pad," is adaptable to inground pools without built-in units or can be used for above-ground pools. This unit usually attaches to the vacuum fitting and may be removed easily.

The skimmer will be most effective when it is located on the down-wind side of the pool; the wind helps the recirculating pump by pushing debris towards the skimmer opening. If the skimmer faces away from the wind, the pump may draw in one direction while the wind blows in another, so that little water passes into the skimmer opening.

Piping the system

The plumbing system is designed to circulate all the water in the pool through the filter system. Normally, water is drawn from the pool from the main outlet and surface skimmer, passes through suction piping to the filter and heater, and then returns to the pool via pressure return lines and inlets.

The main drain is a precast concrete, plastic, or brass sump, 6 to 10 inches in diameter and 6 to 8 inches deep, set in the deepest part of the pool. It serves as a collecting point for debris and draws off dirt that settles to the bottom.

Another intake can be a vacuum line for the vacuum cleaner. But in many pools the vacuum cleaner is attached through the skimmer, eliminating the need for another vacuum line.

Suction and return lines must be of adequate size if the filter system is to operate properly (see chart on page 108). Two or three return lines are recommended, positioned to keep water moving throughout the pool.

Copper pipe (with a minimum wall thickness of Type "L") or plastic pipe (PVC SCH 40 minimum) is almost universally recommended for private swimming pools. Galvanized steel tends to rust and has a short life when buried. For economy, however, galvanized pipe and fittings can be used near the filter, where equipment is subject to regular maintenance.

PIPE SIZES

If galvanized pipe is to be installed, use next larger size. For other variations, check the specification sheet accompanying the filter.

FILTER	GALLONS PER MINUTE	MAIN OUTLET	SKIMMER	VACUUM	OUTLET-SKIMMER-VACUUM COMBINED	RETURN
Sand and gravel	9-15	1¼"	1¼"	1¼"	1½"	1¼"
	15-25	1½"	1½"	1½"	2"	1½"
	21-35	1½"	1½"	1½"	2"	1½"
	29-48	2"	1½"	1½"	2"	2"
High-rate sand and pressure diatomaceous earth	30	1½"	1½"	1½"	1½"	1½"
	40	1½"	1½"	1½"	1½"	1½"
	50	1½"	1½"	1½"	1½"	1½"
	60	1½"	1½"	1½"	2"	1½"
	70	2"	1½"	1½"	2"	2"
	80	2"	1½"	1½"	2"	2"

Plastic pipe has become quite popular. Its low cost, complete resistance to corrosion, good flow characteristics, flexibility, and ease of installation have made it practical for all pool piping. The semi-rigid plastics are joined with special solvent welding compounds and can be formed easily without kinking. Moreover, almost all types of fittings are available for "making up" plastic pipe and joining it to threaded connections.

Some local building codes have not yet accepted plastic pipe, and others accept it only if it carries the National Sanitation Foundation Seal; check the building codes in your area.

HEATING THE POOL

Heating a pool is not mandatory, but even in very mild climates pool heaters are on the increase. They can extend the swimming season from early spring to late fall, or even the year around.

Swimmers generally find water below 70° chilly. Some prefer their swimming water about 75°; most like a comfortable 80° to 84°. But even in the warmest areas, water in unheated pools frequently drops below 70°, even when air temperatures are well above this.

Recently pool heaters have been produced which are "stackless" (presenting a low silhouette and a neater appearance) and have AGA (American Gas Association) all-weather ratings for total outdoor installation. This eliminates the need of a shelter.

Direct heater

Direct heating systems are the oldest type and have moderate initial costs (for a 16 by 34-foot pool, $500-

$650). The gas burners directly heat the boiler pipes carrying the pool water, keeping the operating cost relatively low. In areas where natural gas is not available the heater may be operated by oil or liquid petroleum (LP) gas.

Modern heaters now come with devices that control temperature and velocity of the water in the heat exchanger and thus reduce or prevent scale formation inside the pipes and water condensation outside them. Most modern direct-fired heaters have efficiencies of 80 per cent or more.

Indirect heater

An indirect heater is really two hot water systems in one; the boiler tubes pass through a bath of hot water rather than over direct heat.

There is very little condensation in an indirect system, and scaling is very slow. The complexity of the system makes the initial cost high ($650-$900), but maintenance costs are relatively low. The indirect system tends to keep temperatures of the pool water below the critical point where condensation and scale occur, and cleaning is not required as often as with a direct-fire system. Like the direct-fired heater, the indirect heater can be operated with LP gas or oil.

Alternate methods of heating

Other types of pool heaters have been used with varying degrees of success. The tank type is similar to a household water heater, although it is often much larger. A dome of lime may form on the bottom of the heater and reduce its efficiency, but the low initial cost of these units makes them popular among owners of small pools and above-ground pools.

An elaborate but effective way to heat a pool is by means of copper coils imbedded right in the pool shell. As hot water circulates through the coils, heat is conducted through the pool wall to the water. The system must be installed when the pool is constructed. It consists of a boiler, coils, and a thermostat that automatically activates the boiler when the temperature of the pool water drops below a predetermined level. The coils contain approximately 50 gallons of water. The use of heating coils for pools is relatively new; installation costs are high.

Four-ton electric heat pumps, ordinarily used to heat and cool houses, have also been used to heat residential swimming pools in areas of low electrical rates. However, the plumbing installation must be custom designed, as heat pumps specifically manufactured for pools are not available. Initial costs are considerably more than for a regular pool heater.

The principle of solar heating — using the sun's rays to heat water inexpensively — has long been known. But methods of controlling this heat for swimming pools are far from being perfected. Most solar heating devices now in use were improvised by pool owners with engineering know-how. Since no practical means for storing solar energy has yet been devised, the pool gets no benefit from the heater while the sun is hidden—when heat is usually needed most. But some homemade models, when used for supplementary heating, achieve real economies for their owners.

Heater installation

Since most heaters operate on natural gas, a line must be brought from the main source to the point of installation (figure about $1 a foot); the size of the line depends on the distance involved and the size of the heater.

To eliminate corrosion, all parts of the heating unit should be of non-corrosive materials (copper, brass). The boiler should also have a low-water-pressure safety switch to keep the coils from being fired when no water is passing through them. A control is also needed to shut off the heater if the water gets too hot.

A sensitive thermostat will be the most economical. The best units react to a change of a half degree, while the poorer ones overshoot by as much as 5 degrees before the heater turns off.

What size heater?

Your pool contractor or equipment company will recommend the proper heater size for your pool. Heaters are measured in terms of British Thermal Units. A single BTU is the amount of heat required to raise a pound of water 1 degree Fahrenheit, and heater size is determined by its BTU's per hour.

Because most of the heat from a pool is lost at the surface, the area rather than the gallon capacity of the pool is used to determine the heater required. Multiply the surface area of the pool by 15; then multiply this number by the number of degrees you wish to raise pool temperature above the temperature of the surrounding air. The result will be the BTU's per hour that your pool needs.

For example, if you have a pool with a surface area of 1,000 square feet and you wish it to be 20 degrees warmer than air temperature, multiply 1,000 by 15 by 20. You will need a heater supplying 300,000 BTU's per hour.

Operating costs

The cost of operating a heater depends on the amount of water in the pool and the temperature rise needed to offset daily heat loss. If the pool is used only occasionally and the temperature rise is not great, $15 to $20 a month should cover the costs for a pool about 18 by 36 feet. But in cooler climates, heat costs of $40 to $50 a month are not uncommon.

Don't try to save money by turning the heater on only for weekends or other peak use periods. It costs so much to bring up the temperature of a cold pool that shutting down the heater completely for short periods is false economy. Because the heater is hooked up to the filter system and uses the same pump, it can operate only during the filtering cycle. This may mean that you have to keep the filter running overtime to keep the water temperature at the desired level.

Heat sealants

A heat sealant is a chemical that spreads on the surface of the water to help retain pool heat. A derivative of alcohol, it increases surface tension by forming an invisible layer, only one molecule thick. By reducing losses through radiation and evaporation, the sealant can reduce fuel costs by a third and water costs by half. For every 500 square feet of pool surface, the sealant costs about 50 cents a week.

You can obtain sealant in crystal or emulsion form. It is introduced directly into the skimmer and spreads rapidly over the surface of the pool. When the water surface tension is broken, the layer of sealant quickly reforms; but its effectiveness varies somewhat with the amount of activity in the water. Ordinarily it needs replenishing every 5 or 6 days.

Sealants help cut maintenance costs by holding dirt, leaves, and insects on the surface, so that the skimmer may remove them. Used with an indoor pool, sealants will cut down the steam in the room.

CHECKLIST FOR POOL PLANNERS

A checklist of elements that can be included in a pool area can come in handy when you first sit down to plan the type of swimming pool and accessories you want. The list can be used again when you meet with a builder or contractor to settle on prices and specifications; details on all components can be noted here for comparison with other bids or for later reference in comparing the final contract with first estimates. Those who intend to buy a house with a swimming pool already installed can use the list as a guide to determine if the pool has the best equipment for their purpose.

Details on most of the features included here will be found in the preceding chapters.

POOL STRUCTURE

Size: **Shape:**

Minimum depth   Maximum depth

Longest straight-line swimming distance

Size of diving area

Square footage of water surface

Perimeter   Gallon capacity

Construction material: Poured concrete

Gunite   Hand-packed concrete

Concrete block

Vinyl liner   (with   frame)

Fiberglass   Steel

Other

Steps: Number   Location

Width   Shape

Special areas for children:

EQUIPMENT

Filter: Type

Brand   Size

Pump and motor size

Location of filter, pump and motor

Pipe: Material   Size

Heater: Type

Brand   BTU's

Location   Size

Electrical hookup — Power source

Line length

Gas hookup — Fuel source

Line length

Fittings: Main drain size

Hydrostatic relief valve

Location of return lines

Skimmer size   Skimmer location

Other

Time clock: Location

Hookup

Other features: Special requirements or overloads on circulating system, such as automatic pool cleaner, fountain, waterfall

POOL TRIM

Interior finish: Color

If paint, brand and base

Waterline tile: Size   Color

Decorative tiles   Frostproof

Other tile — Steps   Floor design

Coping: Precast or integral

Color   Texture

Decking: Square footage

Type   Texture

Color   Drainage outlets

Expansion joints

ACCESSORIES

Diving board: Type

Size   Location

Matting

Underwater light: Type

Number   Location

Ladder or grab rails: Inset steps

Location

Life line: Length

Number of floats

Cover: Size   Material

Type of anchor

Other:

MAINTENANCE EQUIPMENT

Vacuum cleaner: Type

Length of hose

Wall brushes: Nylon

Stainless steel   Handle

Leaf skimmer:

Water test kit: Alkalinity

pH   Chlorine residual

Automatic pool cleaner: Type

Pump

Automatic chlorinator: Type

Size

Other:

POOLSIDE STRUCTURES

Fencing: Location

Height   Length

Non-climbable material

Cost per lineal foot

Storage: Maintenance equipment

Accessories

Shelter for filter and pump

Chemicals   Other

Dressing rooms: Number   Size

Location   Shower

Drying area for suits and towels

Outside toilet   Wash basin

Sun shade: Material

Square footage   Support

Wind screen: Location

Height   Material

Sauna: Size   Location

Heater type

POOLSIDE LIVING

Safety: Location of first aid kit

Artificial respiration instructions

List of emergency phone numbers

Safety devices or alarm systems

Pool games: Basketball

Tetherball   Other

Garden games: Equipment

Space required

Paved court: Size   Equipment

Facilities for serving food: Barbecue

Pass-through from kitchen

Snack bar   Drinking water

Refrigerator   Electric outlets

Refuse disposal

Table

Seating for wet people

Seating for dry people

Lights: General illumination

Highlights and special effects

Heat: Fireplace   Firepit

Portable braziers

Radiant heat area   Heat source

Miscellaneous: Telephone

Radio or speaker system for set inside house

INDEX